WHOSE WORLD IS IT ANYWAY?
The Fallacy of Islamophobia

SHAMIS ISMAIL HUSSEIN

This Book is dedicated to
The memory of my Father and Mother,

Contents:

Preface

Since the 11 September 2001 attacks on the Twin Towers in New York, Islam has become ever more widely associated with terrorism. Muslim names, dress code, charities, religious teaching and the educational curricula of some countries have fallen under suspicion. Even the "Hawalah", the traditional means of money transfer, has not escaped controversy. New regulatory measures have been introduced. Furthermore, the proponents of the geopolitical stratifications on democracy and good governance seem to be instigating faith confrontations, which have been critical but not necessarily logical. The world seems to have been polarised and scepticism deepened.

The Bush administration's security measures against real or alleged threats and terror suspects contradict human laws and norms. Therefore, what could have been addressed as specific crime or specific criminals have been generalised to take in a whole community without discrimination and so, intentionally or unintentionally, anti-Islamic sentiments have been propagated.

Despite the fact that many millions of people in the west, (the biggest numbers in the US and UK) demonstrated against the 2003 war on Iraq, marched and campaigned, their leaders remain demagogic. The public has grown ever more disenchanted with their policies on Iraq.

I would like modestly to contribute my view of what one sees as prevailing injustice and Islamo-phobia from the perspective of someone with multiple identities (female, Somali, Muslim, African, Arab affiliated and British citizen). One may be able to subscribe to all these identities knowingly or unknowingly, depending on situations and circumstances, although whichever one is positioned in at any given time undoubtedly dominates the other identities.

As a daughter of a judge, and thus imbued with an egalitarian background, I grew up in an environment with a strong sense of law and justice.

In the course of travelling to and participating in a wide range of conferences, workshops on peace, conflict resolutions, gender equity development and mainstreaming as well as work assignments, I have engaged with many people of different nationalities and different social backgrounds. With that experience and that sense of human relationships, it is possible to enjoy the virtues of universal friendship and to appreciate the endeavours of others.

During my stay in the UK, I have not experienced discrimination or, if I have, have not been aware of and failed properly to pick it up. However, in April 2004, a fellow passenger in a bus in Oxford City asked me why I was wearing a scarf on my head. I replied with a similar sort of question and asked him why he was wearing a tie around his neck. He mumbled and could not give me a satisfactory answer. I wondered what made his piece of material acceptable and mine questionable. It occurred to me that, had he met church-going women with headscarves or even the Queen, who often wears headscarf he would not have asked the same question. At any rate, since 11/09/2001 it has become commonplace for any one wearing Muslim dress or with a Middle Eastern complexion to get at least a second look of a kind that never existed before. Yet, if democracy and freedom of choice are to be maintained, civility is a requirement of personal behaviour. What has made courtesy so scarce these days and why has uniformity become so in favoured?

I undertook the research for this book during my time in Oxford, immediately after the fellowship in International Gender Studies at Queen Elizabeth House Oxford University that enabled me in, the summer of 2004, to finish the book "Women War and Peace: the Somali case". During that period, I encountered much discussion on various discourses, including Islam, the Middle East, cultures, identities, ethnicity and integration amongst scholars, friends and acquaintances. I came to the view that justice was not being done to civilisation outside the western hemisphere and that the approach towards non-western cultures was misanthropic. Islam in particular was greatly misrepresented. I am neither a historian nor a religious expert but, from the little I knew, what was being said did not add up and the sort of Islam that was talked about was not the one I relate to or with which I was brought up. As I have known it, Islam is neither intrusive nor based on hatred of others.

The scale of cultural and religious misrepresentation was enormous; so much so that it triggered my curiosity. Even an amateur can set the record straight. I finished a first draft in September 2005, was busy with another assignment for most of 2006 and then returned to it to prepare it for publication in 2007. Therefore, most of the interviews in this book were compiled in 2005. I would like to express my gratitude to all the friends and acquaintances who have contributed to this work in so many different ways. I am grateful also to the organisers of the International Conference on "Harmony, Conflict Resolution and Reconciliation" at the Indira Gandhi National Centre for Arts in Delhi, India. I greatly value the level of concern and degree of engagement with the global issues and, on a local level, interactions with intellectuals, scholars and practitioners during the conference. The opportunity to discus this essay with my fellow participants was particularly helpful.

So many people of different nationalities have helped me with material, criticism, discussions, encouragement, wisdom and shared passions that it would be a very long list indeed. I have thanked each of them individually and they know who they are, however I owe special debt to Majles Dr. H Ibrahim and http:// passport.Jp of England and Arabia. They both encouraged me to publish this work in a timely manner and sponsored its publication. I am also grateful to Professor John Saeed of Dublin University for editing and suggesting invaluable improvements, Dr. Abdisalam Issa-Salwe Thames Valley University for helping me with the IT. My sincere thanks to all the professionals who read the manuscript or sections of it and made invaluable comments, Jon Snow broadcaster journalist Channel four news London, Professor Modjjaba Sadria of Agakhan University Institute for the study of Muslim Civilizations. Robert Molteno Chairman, publications Committee International African Institute SOAS London, Dr Ibrahim Al-aqidi Research fellow Centre for Islamic Studies Oxford. Taj Kandoura Institute of Oriental studies Oxford University. Mohammed Jalal Sudanese Journalist and writer, Abdallah Homouda Chair of Egyptian Journalists, Abdulahi Hajji Senior producer BBC Somali Service London, Ambassador Timothy Bandora Senior government Adviser Regional Bureau for Africa United Nations programme for development New York   Ultimately, though, the responsibility for mistakes is mine.

The principle aim of this essay is to explore the prevailing contradictions within Islamo- phobia and to animate the perception of how Muslim or Arab communities in the west shifted from being law-abiding citizens to being a menacing danger to the security of an otherwise civilised western world. Other prominent issues that come up repeatedly are: Culture versus economic strategies, democracy, terrorism and the relations between the Horn of Africa and the Middle East. I have given special emphasis to the Horn of Africa dispute, the third party entanglement in it and the impact of the colonial legacy on political-socio economic instabilities in Somalia. Iraq and Palestine, the challenging issues on territorial disputes vis-à-vis religious ideologies and the realities of occupation factors are also brought to attention, including the Palestinian struggle.

Following the disengagement from the Cold War and the collapse of the Soviet Union, critics argue, the invasion of Iraq, weapons of mass destruction, the war on terrorism and so on point towards the ambition of empire-building based on the search for power hegemonies. It was also the case that which seems the Bush administration portrayed the Muslim world as dark corners of the globe that needed to be civilised and liberated. So I briefly describe the situation of present day Iraq, reflected in the history of the country from Mesopotamia and Babylon to Baghdad, pre-modern and contemporary history and how present day western civilisation has triumphed albeit, from Islamic civilisation. Also, the use of religion for political means appears to be a very challenging venture in the context of post-modern power politics. Therefore, with regard to the monotheistic religions, I have emphasised the divergences and convergences between faiths and the dichotomy vis-à-vis faith-related civilisation and contemporary secular societies. The position of women in the religious context is also tackled briefly. Here we find the views and various testimonies of individuals who don't endorse the divisive threats that have risen in today's world and the hate factor.

In the conclusion, topics discussed have been brought together and brief suggestions are made. Finally, it is worth noting that this work has benefited from the views of people from different continents and nationalities. It is not analytic per se. It is more of a factual presentation with an historical perspective. I hope that the book shows a counter-argument to a set of incorrect arguments in order to provide the essential facts behind the hostilities in a single framework that some of the western media have overridden. In essence, the main theme of this work is not to suspend the root cause in order to understand the story behind the headlines, without losing sight for respect and rights of the "other". I have chosen the scope of the debate, not that the Chechens or the Hui Muslims of Xin Jiang in western China, currently being systematically overrun by the Han, and the war in Darfur are less important but that, apart from the limits of my knowledge, I find the nature of crusading war, axis of evil, the super power interventions and contradictions as retardation to human civilisation.

This study is aimed at the non-specialist or general reader. It may also give some insight for specialists and politicians.

Abbreviations

Food and Agriculture Organization (FAO)
British National Party (BNP)
American Enterprise Institute (AEI)
United Nation International Children's Emergency Fund (UNICEF)
Palestinian Liberation Front (PLF)
Union of Islam Courts (UIC)
Somali National Movement (SNM)
Tigra Peoples Liberation Front (TPLF)
Transitional Federal Government (TFG)
Transitional National Government (TNG)
Ogaden National Liberation Front (ONLF)
Western Somali Liberation Front (WSLF)
United Nations (UN)
United States (US)
Union of Socialist Soviet Republic (USSR)
The Combined Joint Task Force Horn of Africa (CJTF-HOA)
United Nations Education Scientific and Cultural Organization (UNESCO)
Project for New American Century (PNAC)
Squad Automatic Weapon (SAW)
Turkish Special Mission (TSM)
International Monetary Fund (IMF)
Central Intelligence Agency (CIA)
US Central Command (CENTCOM)
African Union (AU)
United Nations High Commission for Refugees (UNHCR)

Introduction
Whose World is it anyway?

In the twenty-first century setting, liberal and fair minded people might presume that all battles and wars that have been fought; religious and political, conquerors and converts, liberators and socialists, Maoists, the civil rights movement, as well as other radical movements have been in search of justice and equity within and between nations and groups. All those principled conflicts were expected to lead citizens of the globe to a wiser, fairer and a more just world, but it seems that this has not been the case. Instead, every age presents its strata of domination. Each age has its character and a somewhat distinct mark. In previous civilisations, the majority of rulers have added their own distinctive culture whilst continuing characteristics of the civilisations they encountered. For instance, "The most immediate effect of colonial rule was its impact on the African traders, whose ability to play their traditional late nineteenth century 'monopolistic role as middlemen' was drastically curtailed"[1]. Since then it may be fair to say that structural poverty continues to arrest the development of African continent.

On the issues of globalisation and modernity, the two opposing directions are homogenisation through domination and diversity allowing coexistence. In effect, culture matters a lot to people's identities and it remains persistent around the globe. "For almost no country is homogenous. The world's 200 countries include some 5,000 ethnic groups. Two-thirds of countries have more than one ethnic or religious group making up at least 10% of the population. Many countries have large indigenous populations that were marginalised by colonisation and settlers."[2]. People are very assertive of their cultures and identities and that remains ever more present.

According the United Nations Human Development Report 2004, entitled "Cultural Liberty in Today's Diverse World", "Cultural liberty is a vital part of human development because being able to choose one's identity - which one is - without losing the respect of others or being excluded from other choices is important in

1

leading a full life. People want the freedom to practise their religion openly, to speak their language, to celebrate their ethnic or religious heritage without fear of ridicule or punishment or diminished opportunity. People want the freedom to participate in society without having to slip away from their chosen cultural moorings. It is a simple idea, but profoundly unsettling".[3]

"In modern development, nature and people are treated as resources. These are contested in reality as well as conceptually. In the course of the last fifty years three conflicting trends have shaped research, policies and practices related to resources".[4] The state and the corporate themes of consumerist and economic growth are often opposed by the concerned citizens including environmentalists, scientists and the local communities who basically relate with the natural resources for their living, their traditions and their identities. The corporate state is the most dominating; it uses the multifaceted powers of institutions, including management, technology, money and media backed by force of arms.

The concerned citizens of the world, however, raise awareness of ethics, protection of the earth, cultures of local communities and habitats that are greatly endangered, primarily by developers and the corporate sector. When policies do go wrong between or within states, it is normally the local civilians who suffer most and who are exposed to deprivation.

On the other hand, "in our age the overriding dominance of industry and technology for the material affluence of a privileged minority increasingly drives the preparedness for armed conflict for the protection of the privileged and the keeping the deprived at bay. This conversion of the national and international economies into war systems is not only producing a global war psychosis; it is putting an intolerable burden on the world's given resources and is straining social existence to a breaking-point. Gandhi, reflecting on his English and South African experience, grasped the destructive implications of the modern industrial civilisation for the human spirit and human character."[5]"The starting-point of a Gandhian course of action is this self. The beginning is the simultaneous perception of several duals; the immediate and the internal, the self and the world, the material and the spiritual, the actual and the possible".[6] The most important battle taking place in today's world has two souls, the super-power machine that forces change and pushes to its way and the opposing communities who favour evolved development of a local brand.

There is a sense of urgency at the present time and feelings are running high. The determination for liberty, equality and justice is very pertinent. The outstanding modes and principles are justice for all, responsibility, equality and the sharing of world resources. There is also a need to clarify why the security of one group depends on the insecurity of the other. In other words, what makes it appear that the stability at home depends on the instability of the 'other'? It is also worth re-examining if there are better ways of identifying how to overcome poverty.

The definition of "sharing": Is simply "To use jointly"
In the Somali language there is a saying that defines the following:

"*Aan wax wadaagno waa gar, waxaygaan haysanayaa ee waxaaga haysana waa xaq, waaxayga iyo waxaagabase aan qaato, waali sow maaha*? (Sharing is logical if you keep what is yours and I keep what is mine, that is fair, but to take both is madness).

That is the profound dichotomy in today's phenomenon of fighting over resources, disguised as cultural paradigm and the civilisation factor. Even though the issue of democracy appears to be the focal point in the post cold-war context, the prevailing interdependence of the global economy also underscores the maintenance of world peace and harmony. It is worth noting the comments made by a former Chief Economist of the World Bank, Joseph Stiglitz, who stated that, "the IMF works in the interests of the western capital" in the essay titled 'The hospital that makes you sicker".[7] That order underlines the contentiousness of the so-called free market with the moral imperatives of social justice.

Immanuel Wallerstein, author of "Africa and the Modern World." stated the following about the right policies: "I went down to Washington to participate in a conference called by the Methodist Church on Southern Africa. At lunchtime a lot of Congressmen showed up and I happened to be sitting across from a rather prominent Liberal Republican Senator. He asked me what the conferees thought of Mr. Kissinger's mission. I told him 'not much' and explained why. He then asked me that liberal old question: 'What can the United States do to make sure that it doesn't end this time on the side of the wrong people?' I gave him the only answer I know: 'Get on the side of the right people'.[8] It is also of paramount importance to engage right procedure on its relevant positions in today's world.

Since the collapse of the Soviet Union, Islamo-phobia, stereotypes, regime change, altering the map of the Middle East and democratisation agendas have dominated the mode of the media and current affairs. Post 11/09/2001, the Bush administration emphasised that the world has changed. Militaristic and media campaigns against Muslims have been unleashed. Despite the fact that the west had been familiar with Islam for the past 1400 years, suddenly some of the western media, politicians and commentators behave as if they discovered an unprecedented phenomenon of Islamic threat; a monster at their doorstep. Islam is a dangerous religion, they say. Such expressions as Islamic terrorists, Islamic fundamentalists, Islamic Jihads and Islamic extremists have become the norm for the western-controlled media. The president of the United States of America, Mr. George W. Bush and the Prime minister of the United Kingdom of Great Britain and Northern Ireland, Tony Blair uninhibitedly claimed the world's moral high ground, civilisation supremacy and the duty to extend democratisation and the rule of law to the less fortunate world of Islam and the Arabs. Islam oppresses women, they say. The religion of Muhammad is backward, is echoed. No other prophet or religion be it is Moses or Solomon, Christianity or Judaism has been criticised or demonised as much as the Prophet Muhammad and the religion of Islam. The Arab and Muslim contributions to world advancement have been contested.

When the president of the world super-power says "Islamo fascist", it is by no means a slip of the tongue. To some, however,

4

"Islam equals terrorism" is not a logical equation. Islam as religion does not only promote peace but it is against autocracy.

The scope of this essay includes exploring the drive behind Islamo-phobia. It examines the relations between occupation, invasion and intervention on the one hand and terrorism, insurgencies and Al Qaida on the other. This study reveals how the third party involvement encourages civil strife, sectarianism and clanism, affecting national cohesion. Iraq, Somalia and Palestine are selected as case studies for these current scenarios.

The first part of the book explains the evolvement of traditional democracy in Somalia, the Horn of Africa dispute and the political socio-economic relations between the Middle East and the Horn region. The second section deals with the invasion of Iraq by the coalition of the willing led by the United States and the impact of UN sanctions on Iraqi lives and environment. The Palestinian cause and the beginning of the Israeli occupation in post Ottoman Empire are narrated. Insofar as hate factors fears and assumptions are concerned, sufficient evidence revealing the underlying cause is presented. How the Bush/Blair current wars of pre-emptive nature echo ancient wars of conquest are also expressed in the part on duplicities and contradictions. In the final three parts the contribution of Islamic civilisation to western civilisation is illustrated. In the part on who civilised whom, brief reflection is made on how the west gained invaluable knowledge from Islamic and Arab civilisation. The position of women in Islam in comparison with non-Muslim societies is presented and divergence/convergence between religions is also depicted.

1. Chapter One

Many people do raise the question on what prolonged the Somali civil war and if the Somalis have not been effective in safeguarding the statehood and their national sovereignty. More so neither the Somalis nor the commentator on the Horn failed criticising the Somali clan distinction and blaming it as the major cause of the nation's political disarray. This chapter reflects what undermined the Somalia statehood and the puzzle behind the falling state

1.1 The Impact of Third Party Involvement on Somalia

The Impact of Third Party Involvement on Somalia Democracy and the Middle Eastern Relations with the Horn of Africa:

Many Somalis argue that neither Islam nor the Somali culture embodies oppression and authoritarianism, so infringement of one's choice of governorship has foreign traits. The bulk of the Somali community do believe that the best democracy they encountered is traditional democracy guided by traditional local laws. For that, the democratisation theory in the post-modern period needs to be addressed. Democracy does not mean the freedom to vote or to air one's point of view on radio programmes and television shows. It has much wider implications. The proposition that the western form of democracy is the best type of democracy and how far it would be applicable to non-western societies is also questionable. The tripartite interplay among local traditions, inherited colonial legacies and new models of interventionism needs to be tackled. Somalia could be a case study in this scenario, partly because it is perhaps the only country on the globe that has not had an internationally recognised government for the last fifteen years, was the first African-country to experience colonial aerial bombardment to subdue resistance movements, classified as the only fully homogenous group in sub Sahara Africa and is possibly the first testing ground for the US mission of new world order in the context of peace making and peace enforcement.

Equally Somalia has been perhaps the first testing ground for the humanitarian intervention that indeed differs from humanitarian assistance; hence intervention evokes interpretation and leads to peace enforcement in which the United Nations endorsed the US conditioned 1992 deployment of the 30,800 member US–led United Nation's Task Force to Somalia. It might be the case that Somalia has been one of the casualties of cold war disengagement. For that, it could be a classic example for the tripartite interests, the contrasting paradigms of democracy vis-à-vis tradition and the impact of third party involvement.

1.2 Somali Traditional Mechanisms of Settling Disputes

Case in point: Traditionally Somalis are classified as a democratic and egalitarian society. A *Garad, Boqor, Sultan,Ugaas and Malaaq* title of clan leaders represents clans. Clan leaders are often born orators and are elected on their ability to sway arguments, for their wisdom, wit and knowledge of customary law as well as kinship sociologies and terrain habitats. Clan disputes were/are settled by clan elders, who practice *Xeer* (customary law), which is a blend of traditional and Islamic law. It tackles all issues from the smallest to the largest, including social and criminal matters, guided by unwritten sets of moral values regulated by the traditional social codes. When conflict arises between clans or groups within a clan, the two parties are first expected to engage in negotiations and peace processes under the auspices of the clan council tribunal (*Gurti*) that consists of a judge and jury and is represented by equal numbers from both sides. Should they fail to reach settlement amongst themselves, then and only then would the case be referred to the *ergo* (mediators).

The *ergo* should be independent, chosen for their knowledge of the customary law and expertise on the traditional mechanisms of sorting out clan conflicts. In addition, the conflicting parties must be satisfied that the *ergo* members and venue are to be a neutral quarters approved by the *ergo* members as well. If any one of the adversaries finds the *ergo* verdict not to be satisfactory, then the group states the following: "*Gartaa geed kale -baan ka leeyahay*" (I appeal this verdict to another tree).The tree stands for the assembled council who traditionally use to sit under the shade of renowned trees for sorting out cases. In essence, groups are allowed to appeal against an unfavourable verdict 12 times, and that may vary from clan to clan or in accordance with different regions. They are also expected to specify their concerns and should be convincing enough for the permission to engage further appeals. The final verdict reached by the *ergo* earns utmost respect and is expected to succeed. Clan adversaries can hardly afford to opt against the decisions of the *ergo* for future interactions; more so as the reputation and the survival of the clan, collectively and individually, depend on its adherence to the community laws and social values. In turbulent times clans were honoured not for the number of enemy that they killed but the degree of engagement on war ethics and how they treat the "*Birima-geydo* (forbidden from the sword or harm) including, women, children, elderly, cast groups and the magan groups (those who seek amnesty). No *lib* (victory) derives from harming the *Bir-magaydo* group. On the contrary, failure to protect the vulnerable brings disrepute to the clan and affects future intermarriage with those considered noble clans because the alliance system that is vital in war and in peace draws support also from marriage alliance traditionally based on exogamy practices. In short, the culture provides a set of rules and regulations based on community essence, effective in application and a mechanism of deterrence. Therefore traditional pillars of kinship in *xeer* (customary law), *Soyaal* (classic) and *Ugub* {jurisprudence} as well as monotheistic religious beliefs (Islam) are predominantly the foundation of the social fabric. That supplies people with a framework that gives meaning and direction for life. It is dynamic, constantly revised, accommodating and, given the opportunity, provides individuals the will to understand other cultures. Would that, therefore, be regarded as "absence" of democracy? Or is it not worth considering the relationship between dictatorship, totalitarianism and the post-independence modern state system that principally derived from colonial inheritance and global integration? That does not mean there were no locally produced tyrants, but that the then existing traditional methodologies were equipped to tackle local problems. Nonetheless, it was during the colonial period that regional and local balance of power was disturbed. The parts of Somalia where there is peace today are those invoking the customary laws.

Furthermore, Somalis are renowned for their use of poetry, the art of wit and the composition of plays in expressing their thoughts and views in politics, reconciliation processes, settling scores in war-time, peace promotions and individual endeavours in love, in joy or in despair. Described by professor B.W.Andrzejewski, who was an authority on Somali and other Cushitic languages in the Horn of Africa, perhaps nowhere else in the world is poetry so frequently used in expressing all aspects of people's lives as is the case in Somalia.

Richard Burton also commented about it. Burton, the British explorer and the author of "The First Footsteps in East Africa" stated the following: "The country teems poets, poetasters, poetitos, poetaccios, Every man has his recognised position in literature as accurately defined as though he had been reviewed in century of magazines-the fine ear of this people causing them to take the greatest pleasure in harmonious sounds and poetical expressions, whereas a false quantity or prosaic phrases excite their violent indignation"[9]

Therefore, the local people record and express in poetry all the political changes that Somalia has experienced from colonial to superpower involvement to post-modern times and so on.

1.3 Foreign intervention on Somalia and the Horn of African relations with the Middle East.

Having given you (the reader) a glimpse of a side of Somalia that is hardly mentioned outside the Somali sphere, it is worth exploring the constraint that hugely upsets Somali society and what has linked Somalia to today's terrorism phenomenon.

Again, it is all about economics. According to Lord Mountnorris of Britain who visited the Horn of Africa, at the turn of the nineteenth century Britain was to occupy Aden to get access to the then trade of Somalia in Berbera as the following quotation explains; "A private English expedition under Lord Mountnorris visited the red Sea and one of its members, Henry Salt, was sent into Abyssinia from Massawa, while Salt was in Abyssinia, Mountnorris explored the coast of the Aden and the Red Sea and the Gulf of Aden, visiting Mocha, Aden and Berbera. He discovered a very large annual market, or fair as it was called, at Berbera, and in 1808 he urged the British government to occupy Aden, in order to exploit the trade of Berbera."[10] Since then Somalia was partitioned and repartitioned among the European powers at different times, but in particular, Britain gave segments of Somali territories to the neighbours in Ethiopia and in Kenya. In one instance the British officer in Moyale (Somali inhabited, present day northern province of Kenya) encountered mosquitoes, so he then changed once again the boundary demarcation between Somali and Kenya accordingly.

In the case of Ethiopia, prior to the colonial period the word Ethiopia was to be found in Biblical works in which the Greeks referred to the black people in the region including the Sudan and Libya. The Abyssinian proper, who are predominantly Christian, politically dominant but numerically one of the minorities in Ethiopia, were told to take part in the partition of the region, including Somali territories, the Afar and the Oromo's, who comprise the majority of present day Ethiopia.

Be that as it may, the then European powers in the region entered into more territorial concessions with the Abyssinian leaders, in particular the Amhara. As Mr. Rodd of Britain states in a letter to Lord Salisbury after ceding a segment of Somali territory to king Menelik of Abyssinia, "In a view of the great difficulties I have had to encounter, including moral pressure, while the French had but a few weeks ago accepted so conspicuous a curtailment of their protectorate claims on the Somali coast, I trust that your Lordship will consider that the arrangement is as satisfactory one as we are entitled to expect"[11] The view of the then British authorities that has been repeatedly quoted in modern politics was that Abyssinia is an island surrounded by a "Muslim sea". What is not often mentioned is that Christianity was introduced to the Abyssinians by Arab Christians from Yemen and Syria, continuously assisted by Egyptian churches in Alexandria. The Abyssinian languages derived from the Arabian language of Gees origin from Yemen. Generally speaking, the people of the Horn of Africa are from the same racial stock and have experienced similar waves of migration and interaction for most periods of their history. Ethiopian Christians gain respect and peace pacts from the Muslim world. During the Muslim rule in Jerusalem they were exempted from taxation by the Muslim rulers of the time. Thus, there are many cultural and ethnic similarities embodied in the relics of the region. With the right policies, therefore, one could point out the availability of unifying factors by excising the readiness of conflict hardening in the region; more so while present-day Ethiopia is a Christian state although it believed that the majority of the Ethiopian people are, in effect, Muslims. The religious distinction has not been very significant. Hence the same family could be comprised of both Muslims and Christians. However, in the ensuing battle of divide and rule, the Abyssinians were led to believe that Menelik II of Abyssinia was descended from King Solomon, the story being embodied in the historical religious studies of the love affair between King Solomon and the Queen of Sheba. In reality however, there has never been a Menelik I and titles like Haile Sellassie, Theodore's and Menelik are acquired as one becomes king in the then Abyssinia. This story of Queen Sheba, known to the Yemenis as "Balqis" often embarrasses Abyssinian scholars and other knowledgeable people in present-day Ethiopia who are aware of the regional story because it is a story shared among others with the Southern Arabian people. But the Abyssinian Queen of Sheba lingers and, indeed, is entertained more by foreigners then is the case among the Ethiopians.

What is unique about Ethiopia or, to be precise, Abyssinia is that it is perhaps the only African country into which European missionaries didn't introduce Christianity. It is rather striking that the Syrians, who are hardly mentioned, built the famous religious sites of Ethiopia. However, the European colonial powers allied with the Abyssinian kings (in particular the Amhara kings) against the other ethnic groups inside Ethiopia as well as neighbouring Somalia. The British in particular not only divided Somali territories but played a role in fuelling clan disputes to undermine Somali unity while supporting Emperor Haile Sellassie of the Amharas, as the following statement revealed, made during a conference in Harar (Somali claimed region ruled by Ethiopia) between the British officials in Somaliland and the Ethiopian authorities of the time, detailed by J.R.Stebbing, Chief Secretary to the then Government of the Somaliland protectorate: "The Ethiopian official policy towards the 1954 agreement and has the support of every member of the Somaliland protectorate delegation (British officers in the then Somaliland) is this: To reduce grazing rights by cultivation and to encourage settlements by Ethiopian tribes, or persons they can claim as Ethiopians, wherever the rainfall and soil conditions are suitable;... (v) To obstruct and (incidentally humiliate) the protectorate tribal leaders of those tribes to which they lay such claim... (vii) To split the potential alliance of Somali peoples against them, by fostering the traditional antipathy between the Issaq and the Darood groups of tribes …. The Somaliland protectorate members of the delegation (British authorities) were also agreed that Ethiopian policy towards the Somalilands is undoubtedly expansionist and imperialistic... my own view is that the wider Ethiopian policy will be to split the Somali people in such a way that hopes of any great Somali federation will be frustrated …This policy will also have the advantage of enabling the Emperor to escape the fear of encirclement by Islam…. As the right of H.M.G. in order to reach a proper understanding of the meaning of the exchange of Notes following the 1954 Agreement: it seems to me that H.M.G has the right to insist on this as a natural corollary to having accepted the note after the signing of the agreement ."[12]

This attitude has not altered in the postcolonial period but procedures and methodologies have varied amongst external actors in the regions.

The only time those British politicians advocated the unity of all Somalis (with the exception of former French Somaliland) was during the post Second World War period when Britain aimed not to give back to Italy territories captured when Mussolini was defeated. Even then the British authorities were economically motivated. The most irrigated parts of Somalia in the south at the riverbanks are regarded as the 'food basket of the country' by economists.

During the de-colonisation period the former British Protectorate and former Italian colony of Somalia united and formed the then Somali Republic. Such unity was a symbol of the search for a greater Somalia and the aspiration that all Somali speaking territories needed to be sharing one flag. The arguments were to liberate the rest of the Somalis under the rule of non-Somali bodies, i.e. French Somaliland (present day Republic of Djibouti} and the two adjacent parts to Kenya and Ethiopia. The new Republic of Somalia therefore concentrated in building a strong army culminating in unprecedented nationhood consciousness and an articulated campaign of national irredentism. The French, for their part, changed the name of French Somaliland to "The Land of the Issas and Afar" in 1967.

The majority of the Afars are to be found in Ethiopia and are regarded as ethnically the closest to the Somalis, whilst the Issas are the major Somali clan in Djibouti. Nevertheless the interpretation was that the French were to play down the significance of Djibouti as a Somali land by changing its name. Consequently the Somali Republic was burdened with the grievances of other Somalis. Because of colonial divisions and boundary demarcations, clans inside the Republic were separated from their other kinsmen as well as pasture lands .This fuelled Somalia's confrontations with her neighbours, in which as early as 1963 the Ethiopian and Kenyan governments of the time signed a joint treaty of defence against Somalia. In such a scenario, the impact of the colonial legacy has been enormous and continues to affect regional peace. As a Somali proverb says, *ayax teeg eel se reeb* (the Locust is gone but has left behind the eggs). Therefore colonial legacies are affecting regional peace. In the other dimension, when African groups in Casablanca and Monrovia contested the colonial inherited boundaries because an immediate revision would avoid boundary disputes, the decision made was to leave colonial

13

boundaries as inherited lest some countries cease to exist. Ironically, when Somalia was seeking to bring all Somali speaking territories under one flag they were accused of being expansionists who should accept the colonial inherited boundaries. When the Majority of the people of the former British protectorate dissolved the union as the security of the South Somalia former Italian colony deteriorated, they too were accused as secessionists.

In the post-independence years, US policy in the Horn was not very different from that of the UK during the colonial period. Subsequently, the US established a base in the then Ethiopia. "The American–Ethiopian Agreement of 1953 on Mutual Security Guarantees" concerned the preferential supply of assistance by the USA to the armed forces of Ethiopia and the guarantee of "certain American interests," first and foremost of which was the operation of the centre of communication in Asmara, which was of great importance at the time…"[13]

In the events of international politicking, manoeuvring and counter manoeuvrings, present day Ethiopia is regarded as the traditional ally to the US and Israel against Yemen, the Sudan and Somalia. The minority Abyssinian groups are also supported to keep a lid on the aspirations of the majority of the people in present day Ethiopia, including the Oromas as well as the Afars, Somalis and others under their jurisdictions.

During the Cold War, the then Soviet Union was an ally of Somalia. The Chinese and other Eastern Block countries were also supportive in development, infrastructure and the building of Somali Army forces. The country was progressing in various fields including education. According to UNESCO, Somalia was 7th position in mathematics on the world education record in the 1970's and the then Somali army was described as the fourth largest, best-trained army in sub Sahara Africa. However, the upshot of the story was when Somalia waged war against Ethiopia in July –August 1977. Initially she gained all her territories back from Ethiopia in the 1977-78 war on the Horn of Africa, but two protagonists(Ethiopia and Somalia) were both under the influence of the then Warsaw Pact. Subsequently Somalia lost the war, not because Ethiopia was able to strike back but because of the combined military involvement from the then eastern block led by the then Union of Socialist soviet Republic (USSR), as the following quotation explains: "The decision by Moscow and Havana to come to Mengistu's rescue became evident between November 1977 and February 1978 as Soviet planes and ships transported roughly 15,000 Cuban troops and large supplies of Soviet weapons and a USSR military mission led by Gen. Vasilii I. Petrov helped direct Ethiopian–Cuban military activities. The massive Soviet–Cuban airlift spurred an Ethiopian counter-offence, which evicted Somali forces from the Ogaden and entrenched the Mengestu regime in power..."[14]

At the time both Yemen and Libya were also under the influence of then Soviet Union. They were in the battlefield with Ethiopia against Somalia, in which their brotherhood in socialism was a higher priority for them than Somalia's Arab League membership or the Islamic factor!

As a result, ambitions for greater Somalia have been shelved, followed by the upsurge of domestic instability. What is even more ironic is the role of the then US administration in the Somali civil war as the following quotation explains: "US military assistance valued at about $1.4 million arrived on June 28, 1988 at the port of Berbera. The lethal arms came at a critical point in the war and were used to regain control of the land, including Hargeisa, which the SNM controlled from May 31 to July 13, 1988. Furthermore, in a controversial action that had the effect of boosting the Somali government's military capability in the northern war zone, an American military team repaired the Somali army's communication site at Hargeysa, which was damaged in the fighting. US policy appeared to reinforce Siyad Barre's harsh retaliation...as result the SNM and the Issaq clan was badly shaken by the ferocity of the government response."[15] When Somalia was fighting against Ethiopia, the US not only warned the then government of Somalia not to attack Ethiopia, but it failed to deliver promised weaponry. Paradoxically, however, it did not exercise the same restraint when it happened to be a Somali against Somalia.

However, the Somali State disintegrated and the centre failed to hold. The overthrow of President Barre's regime followed by the then power struggle amongst opposition groups devastated Somalia by and large. The intervention of the US Marines controversy over the Restore Hope mission contributed further instability. The persistence of the warlords ravaged most of southern Somalia. Nonetheless, against all odds, and with a very little aid from the international community, the Somali people exhibited resilience with informal business ventures and community provisions. Thus appears the dynamic vis-à-vis the community, the nation, the 19th century modern state apparatus, impact of the colonial legacies and the effects of third party involvements including the superpower conflict in the Horn.

On a regional level, explicitly or implicitly, both Ethiopia and Kenya have expressed their reluctance to see a strong Somalia once again. The then president of Kenya Daniel Arap Moi, stated in a speech at an American university and later broadcast by the BBC Somali Service, Bush House, London, that even though there are Somali peace talks hosted by Kenya, the truth is that Kenya would not like to see a united strong Somalia once again. The general understanding is that Somalis are capable and, should they get their way, they would be a "threat" to the region. Nevertheless, what is yet to be articulated is how far Somalia's neighbours threaten her stability and why the terms "threat" and "fear" are so nurtured instead of peace and reconciliation.

A Somali woman from Mogadishu, who attended almost all the peace talks on Somalia in Addis Ababa, Republic of Djibouti and Kenya, stated the following: "Personally I think it is some of the external actors whether regional or international, who are obstacles to the likelihood of Somali state. In Mogadishu today there are a lot of 'conspiracies theories'. My argument is, if Somaliland were to be recognised because of her stability;

A) The Somali name would have been saved in the international scenarios to avoid the absence of statehood.

B) In the South that action might have expedited finding a solution, whether to open a dialogue with our Somali brothers in the North and suggest the capital to be in Hargeysa instead of Mogadishu, or to engage reconciliation within the South and then talk to the peaceful parts of Somalia afterwards. In effect, lessons would be learnt from Puntland and Somaliland. Indeed, look for a Somali solution within, as well as seeking support from the right groups in the international community especially those who don't have a vested interest... personally I do not endorse the building blocks that some seem to advocate."

Since the above-mentioned interview was taken, the situation in the south has changed drastically and the Islamic Courts defeated the warlords, who were substantially supported by some groups within the US administration. Originally the Islamic Courts were founded by a group of businessmen who wanted to bring law and order and their gunmen became Mogadishu's strongest army force. The warlord structure that prevailed in Mogadishu and the near regions for more then 15 years has been replaced by the Islamic courts. In the period during which the warlords were privileged in Mogadishu, the region was characterised as chaotic and insecure. The Islamic courts brought security and accountability with them. They opened the Mogadishu seaport and airport that had been affected by the protracted civil strife. The Union of Islamic Courts (UIC) preceded to most parts of the southern regions with much less bloodshed. Basically, they were welcomed by the public, who were adamantly against the USA supported warlords.

The UIC are comprised of thre e types. First are those who introduce massive restrictions and less tolerance, whose heightened language could arouse opposition. Second are those who accommodate the scholarly sober Sunni tradition that, whilst a Muslim should observe Islamic commands with sincerity, that a believer is also expected to be considered as human and can hope for guidance and forgiveness from Allah Almighty. Their doctrines are based on giving a space to education and they express the Shari'ah with a tone of progress, discipline and enlightenment that attracts the national tradition across the spectrum. The third group is geared towards political empowerment and legitimisation of their concepts through the popularity of the Islamic courts but are not prominent in national politics.

Nonetheless, the emergence of the Somali Union of Islamic Courts in Mogadishu and the success they brought with them triggered an appetite for igniting regional war. One would expect that, if the Union of Islamic Courts brought peace to their region, they would be commended. The concerns upon the long tradition of Somali secularism and any related misgivings, as well as the pros and cons of such an episode should have been debated in a more stable condition. Instead of giving a space for talks between the Somali Transitional Federal Government, formed in Nairobi under the adjudication of the international actors and the Union of Islamic Courts locally branded, a diplomatic outcry and a move to full scale war was prompted. The Bush administration forwarded a resolution that would enable the arms embargo on Somalia to be lifted. The US Ambassador to the United Nations, John Bolton said, "Not intervening was not an option". Subsequently, the US-led resolution was adopted unanimously by the 15 nation Security Council. The Security Council Resolution backs sending an African force of 8000 to support Somalia's weak government and the easing of an arms ban to let the government re-arm. The spokesman for the union of the Islamic courts, Mr. Adow gave an interview to the BBC Network Africa in London UK, on December 7, 2006 and said the following, "Supporting the government, which only controls the area around the town of Baidoa (some 250km, miles to the west of Mogadishu.), would create more trouble and complications in Somalia…Deploying foreign forces to Somalia is seen as invading forces and the Somali people are prepared to defend against aggression". The very questions that have been raised by observers are: "Why does the UN want to go in now that the Islamists have done a better job than that of any foreign interventionists and what need for the UN in taking sides between two Somali groups?" US Ambassador to Ethiopia, Professor David Shinn's report, forwarded by John Mbaria, on East Africa, October 23, 2006 says the following: "Since the defeat of the warlords and the rise of The Union of Islamic Courts, there has been a significant increase in outside engagement," and accuses some of the countries of "meddling". It lists 12 countries that are playing direct and indirect roles in the conflict and bankrolling either the Transitional Federal Government (TFG) or The Union of the Islamic Courts (UIC). The report tries to justify why Ethiopia went into Somalia. It says that Ethiopia and Somalia engaged in a protracted military conflict in 1977/78 over Ogaden, which constitutes 25 percent of Ethiopia's total land area. Whilst prone to drought, the area is rich in natural gas and has up to four million Somali inhabitants. Prof Shin says, "Addis Ababa worries that a hostile government in Mogadishu would strongly support Ogaden National Liberation Front (ONLF) and Western Somali Liberation Front (WSLF). (Somali opposition groups inside Ethiopia)... The report says that the US role, on the other hand, is driven by concern over the entrenchment of fundamentalism in the country and its possible spread to the region...Since early this year the US had committed substantial financial resources to arming the warlord..."

However, that has been described by Le Monde Diplomatique as a "policy blunder," in that it earned the Islamists nationalistic support from ordinary Somalis. John Mbaria, concluded that the "belief is... the US unwittingly fuelled the rise of the Islamists and by wanting to bring friends and foes for an anti-Islamists assault, it could actually foment a serious international conflict".

When it comes to the Horn of Africa, the US engages Ethiopia as the caretaker of the region. As early as October 1992, during the "hundred day action plan" on Somalia, among the members of the international community including governmental and non-governmental organisations and agencies that took place in the UN at Geneva, the US representative suggested that the Somali peace talks be hosted in Ethiopia. The Egyptian spokesman advocated that, even though Somalis and Ethiopians share a lot and in many ways are close people, nevertheless the Somalis are very proud people and their dignity and integrity should be respected at the time of their weakness and, since Ethiopia and Somalia engaged in war, it is not ideal to bring

Somali peace talks under Ethiopian auspices. The Egyptian option was declined. Since then the Ethiopian government has continued to play an active role in Somali politics. Whilst the US led United Nations Forces on Somalia departed, the Ethiopian forces were unofficially operating and intervening in certain parts of Southern Somalia at various times. As opportunity presents itself, the Ethiopian government wages a full-scale war, on the ground and in the air against Somali's UIC in the Southern regions. Consequently, on December 25th 2006, Mogadishu airport and Ballidoogle airport were bombarded. On Christmas Eve, the Ethiopian prime minister admitted sending his army into Somalia to defend the Transitional Government against what he calls "this terrorist" and added, "Our forces and that of the transitional federal government have broken the back of the international terrorist forces…" The US could not wait for the Ethiopians to do the job for them. They too engaged in aerial bombardment on parts of Southern Somalia. One US commentator said that the Ethiopians were unorganised. From another angle, therefore, what are the principle links of terrorism to Somalia, the Horn of Africa and the Middle East?

With regard to the relations between the Horn of Africa and the Middle East, this goes way back to ancient times. For instance, according to some historians and journalists including Anis Mansur (an Egyptian historian and journalist for October Magazine), the ancient Egyptians were said to have come from the Land of the Somalis and were possibly the first to settle the Nile. Furthermore the ancient Egyptians are said to have referred to Somalia as the "Land of Gods and Ancestors". Also, the Semitic influence in the Horn of Africa is substantial, much dictated by the geographical proximity. The extension of the Red Sea, which divides Arabia from Africa itself, marks the geological rift that starts with the Jordan Valley and the Dead Sea, leading to the Wadi Arab and the Bay of Aqaba at the head of the Red Sea. Thus Somalia lies at the south of the Gulf of Aden. Some western journalists and government members often suggest that Somalia is a poor country and that the latest grave escalations owe much too international neglect. It is counter-argued that in effect Somalia has never been left alone by the powers of modern times. Since the collapse of the state and the ousting of the Socialist regime of Mohammed Siyad Barre on January 1991, there appeared an opportunity for unprecedented interventionism of all sorts. From a Somali point of view, the likelihood of vocalising Somali state has been constantly hampered. For example, when the then North West Somalia/Somaliland implemented a locally mediated and funded administration, there was no assistance forthcoming from the international community and they often blamed as secessionists. The transitional federal government that was formed in Nairobi did not gain concrete support for the first two years, and the Union of the Islamic Courts were attacked outright just as they brought peace to a beleaguered community that had not seen stability for more then 15 years. Only when the Islamists gained the local people's respect did the transitional federal government attract foreign support. Moreover, there is a general belief among Somalis that they have been subjected to unofficial international sanctions of a diverse nature and that the US administration winks and whispers to governments that it has influence on to restrict their trade relations with Somalia. Persons of cross clan and region said that the ban on the Somali passport, Somali livestock and the discouragement of bilateral aid and investment all contribute to the delay in the formation of a central state that marks tacit economical and political sanctions against the Somali people. The US forces are said to be present in the coastline of the Somali territorial waters, both in the Gulf of Aden and in the Indian Ocean, in the name of security and combating terrorism. Somalia is Mr. Bush's axis of evil list.

The closure of the major local Hawalah, 'Baraket', has been a tremendous setback to local informal economy. The Baraket Hawalah was found during the interruption of the Somali national banking system and gained its popularity when the state infrastructure collapsed as a means of informal banking system based on community norms of money transferring and investing. Again, disruption of the local economic initiatives, local knowledge with no sufficient provisions or alternatives, is one of the stumbling blocks of North South economic paradigms. For example, when the Baraket Hawalah offices were closed because of the USA instigation in its linkage with terrorism, the US failed to provide evidence that could prove Baracket's involvement with terrorist finances or dealings. In particular, some Swedish lawyers came forward in defence of the Baraket's local office in Sweden. Subsequently Baraket made its files available for further investigation and it is said to have been cleared of any wrongdoing. Nonetheless, the damage was done and the Western Union overtly began to collude with other Somali Hawalah (e.g. Dahab-Sheel) for regulator and legitimisation purposes. Questions that arise out of these scenarios are what makes someone's financial bodies legitimate and others illegitimate or illegal and why some are licensed to handle other people's financial affairs and others are deterred so frequently, instead of corporations and mutual exogenesis between nations and people. If poverty is to be alleviated in Africa (let alone making it history) wouldn't it be plausible to change policies that attribute poverty rather then to promote aid and create more dependence?

As for Somalia being a 'poor country', it is certainly poor in political stability but rich in various resources. Several studies confirm that the Somali territories are oil and gas rich. Among others, the World Bank and the United Nations Development Programme undertook a regional hydrocarbon study that was financed by the UNDP in cooperation with the governments of France, Britain and Canada and some oil companies as late as 1988. According to the World Bank, Somalia also rears one of the world's largest supplies of livestock. The composition of agricultural and fishery strongholds is known. Most of all, Somalia's geographical location attracts political economists. Abdirahman Elmi, Director-General for the Somali Ministry of Agriculture 1965-73 and general manager of the national Petroleum Agency from 1973-1978, also stated the following, "The large reserves of petroleum in Somalia are well known to international oil companies. I was told by some authorities these quantities are reserved for future use as need be" and added "Somalia is far from being poor, apart from the agricultural areas of the south in the coast of Somaliland/North West Somalia, due to the watershed system of the coast, these huge reservoirs of ground water on the coast from west and east the quantity in these areas can be easily utilized for Agriculture and horticulture and will generate hard cash as export commodity"

During the colonial period, the Horn of African par-politics was lumped with that of the Middle Eastern political caveats and, if the curse in the Middle East has been somewhat oil, that of the Horn of Africa may have been primarily the region's 'geopolitical importance'. Hence Somalia is situated at the crossroads of three continents; Asia, Africa and Europe. Because of her strategic location, Somalia has been a vantage point for political strategists in many ways. The word "strategy" is profoundly related to economic, military, moral, psychological and scientific developments.

The emergence of the US as a mono-power exacerbates America's further involvement in the region. Paradoxically, therefore, the issues of terrorism, Horn of African and Middle East appeared to be interlocutors. According to the report of the World Peace Foundation on combating terrorism in the Horn of Africa, Yemen, Djibouti, Eritrea, Kenya, Somalia, and the Sudan: "the countries constituting the Horn of Africa - together with Yemen, are [considered] potential hostages to terrorism…"[16]

The post-modern political-socio economic strategists seem to be engulfed by the terrorism phenomenon, as the following quotation indicates: "Roughly 1400 US military personal thus oversee a region that encompasses [the Horn and Yemen] and coastal waters of the Red Sea, Gulf of Aden and the Indian Ocean. CJTF-HOA (The Combined Joint Task Force Horn of Africa) is based in Djibouti, in part because of its location on the Bab al-Mandeb Strait, the second busiest shipping lane in the world and a potential conduit for terrorist activity"[17]. While the USA is present in Somali territorial waters, in some cases without the consent of local inhabitants, according to the following quotation the US strategic alliance in the Horn region seems to be in line with that of the European powers in nineteenth century: "… the U.S. has some leverage with Ethiopia because Ethiopia benefits from the East African Counter Terrorism Initiative and the U.S 'Terrorist Interdiction

Program'. Ethiopia and Washington share a close personal relationship, with an array of official visits to discuss terrorism, and experts urged continuing engagement. Ethiopia officially supported US efforts in Iraq..." [18] It added, "In return, Ethiopians are interested in counter terrorism help in dealing with Somalia where there are legitimate terrorist concerns...Ethiopia must bear the primary responsibility for dealing with counter terrorism. The U.S. doesn't have the language or cultural skills to deal with these problems".[19] It continued, "Since 9/11, when U.S. counter terrorism efforts became engaged more actively in Somalia the U.S. has had to rely on intelligence from Ethiopian sources..."[20] One of the participants of the Harvard conference who is an "expert" observed that Ethiopia does not believe a Somali state would be in its interest and asked, "Have we used Ethiopia or have they used us?." [21] Furthermore, in the same conference in Harvard, an "expert" described Kenya as "America's strongest partner in the global war on terrorism and its most stable and reliable ally in the Horn and East Africa region." [22]

All-in-all Somalia could be a case study for the dynamics and interplay of culture and community on one hand and par-modern state and interventionism on the other hand. Some Africanist scholars and analysts argue that the present day Somali experience might be a fate waiting for the rest of Africa. Nevertheless, in a world where the flux of power seems to undermine the art of diplomacy and negotiations, it is vital to regain government institutions to protect national resources and interests.

However, the micro and macro models of civil strife depend very much on the cultural relics, saturated characteristics of each nation and the degree and the nature of foreign intervention. For instance, in the case of Somalia, one of its major advantages that enable Somalis to overcome certain obstacles has been the existence of vibrant community networks that operate across clans. Also, clanism has its positive and negative aspects depending on situations and circumstances. Daniel Arap Moi, former president of Kenya, commented many times on television and radio by warning the Kenyans that they are not like Somalis and would not survive a week if civil war erupts in Kenya. In a meeting at Sheraton in Addis Ababa on October 2002 about Somalia and its current status, one Ethiopian expert also commented that, if the same thing should have happen to Ethiopia, they (The Ethiopians) may not survive more then few weeks. One Ethiopian taxi driver stated the following about Somalia's stateless situation: "Somalis are by nature entrepreneurs but we are not. They maintain this attitude of trust and approachability, we don't. Because of our feudalistic background people are hesitant whereas the Somalis easily help one another even if their clans are fighting back home. Many persons from my region travelled to the stable regions of Somalia to gain business expertise and knowledge. There has been a government farm in Ethiopia where we used to rear Somali sheep that have the black neck to exchange hard currency with the Arab countries who prefer the Somali sheep during the Iid-Al Adha …Our prime minister told us to learn the good things from them but not the bad things like clannishness and chewing qat."

Therefore, whilst the strength of the Somalis has been community coordination, networks and a culture of resilience, their experience of foreign intervention statehood has not been one of a good record. An elderly Somali says the following: "There is no doubt that some Somalis have failed us in not solving their problems. And I refer to those who keep on shuttling from one capital to another for the so-called mediations and formation of government, as there is no excuse for that; on the other hand, who is encouraging them and who are the facilitators? The majority of Somali territories are peaceful and they don't receive the same publicity. Also, since the collapse of the central state more priority has been given to report writing and I believe that we have been over researched, but if those funds were directed in to institution building and development, that would have contributed to state building. A question that remains unanswered, at least from our part, is: If Operation Restore Hope was to save lives, how did it turn into bloody war? Another puzzle is why Somalia is always in the hot key spots, considering that we are a small nation and war ravaged one. All of this adds up that foreign intervention contributed the absence of a central state even though we are partly to be blamed". When asked if Somalia is a threat to the security of neighbouring countries and that of others, he replied: "That is simply out of the question. I would say that Somalia has never been more vulnerable then she is now, let alone terrorising others, and I am 90 years of age. I think the reverse is the case and I do not see a spokesperson for that yet but, as believer, one never loses hope. Wisdom is that one should always look for the brighter side regardless... "

It is also believed that some governments and warlords deliberately jumped on the bandwagon of the fight against terrorism for their own political gains with regard to regional and local conflicts. In the Harvard conference one expert related a conversation with Prime Minister Meles Zenawi of Ethiopia: "[Meles] said, we don't look at this as us joining the U.S. on the war on terrorism, we see it as the U.S. finally joining us because we've been victims for many years".[23]

In this context there is pressing need to differentiate terror and terrorists from existing local and regional grievances. The Ogaden region of Somalia among other communities in the present day Ethiopia were incorporated in to the Ethiopian empire of Menelik II in 1897 by the British administration of the time. Therefore, to call Oromo's or the Ogadeni Somalis and other opposition groups' terrorists is an evaded duty to the promotion of democracy and equity between nations and within a nation. The word terrorism is regarded as violence, aggression, dread, dismay, awfulness, hostility, intimidation, fright and evokes interruptions to normality be it individual, communities or states. For that, certain groups within Ethiopia's heterogeneous communities plus Somalis in the wilderness do argue that their political socio-economic choices and aspirations are constantly disrupted. That does not only qualify as terrorism but it also contradicts the principle virtue of self-determination and freedom of choice. It is worth noting one of the common tales expressed across Somali speaking territories. The local anecdotes include that the colonial powers, in particular the then British authorities in the region, were not only divisive, but were also economically disruptive factors to the nomads and the pastoralists. Needless to say, livestock and animal husbandry was/is the backbone of local economies. Similarly in the post-colonial period, the western mode of aid and assistance has not been compatible with local priorities. Bringing solutions without consultation prompts hindrance to pastorals as well as agriculturalists. Because, in the nomadic areas, the mode of aid encourages urbanisation and disruption of animal husbandry, it influences local patterns of rumination and evolvement. The food aid program also affects the local harvest through the selective timing of food distribution. That consequently discourages local production, self-sufficiency and self-reliance. Stabilising and establishing positive relations with the region requires willingness to accommodate local initiatives, cultures and practices; as well as choices and deliberations.

During Meles Zenawi's visit to the U.K on February 2003 at Chatham House the Royal Institute of International Affairs in London, I asked Prime Minister Zenawi if his administration had been politically and economically capitalising, maximising and taking advantage of Somalia's weakest stage. I gave him the example of coffee farms replaced by qat cultivation, since the Somalis are the major customers for qat consumption and mentioned the view that the U.S. supports a "Greater Horn" regional status lead by Ethiopia. In his reply, Mr. Zenawi admitted that qat has been more profitable to local farmers and that competition for the coffee market has been high. The Prime Minister then gave an overview of the relations between the two peoples and the refugee issues. Despite its length, the answer was very diplomatic but, in a nutshell, the Prime Minister indicated that his administration inherited much of Ethiopia's political position and regional arrangements and that it wouldn't be easy to discard it so soon. During Somalia's heyday, Mr. Zenawi benefited from the amnesty of the then Somali government and was holder of a Somali passport. One of the distinguishing marks that the 1977-78 Ethiopian Somalia war left behind has been its impact on internal regional political settings and integration between the two peoples. Dr. Ahmed, a Somali Ethiopian in Switzerland whose doctorate thesis has been about the Horn of Africa, expressed his views and stated: "There are so many factors that are hardly addressed. For example, Somalia lost the physical side of the war because of the intervention of the then Soviet Union and her allies, but Somalia has effectively contributed in liberating the hearts and the minds of the people in the region in multiple ways. Different ethnic groups of Ethiopians; e.g. Oromo's, Tigre Afar, some Amhara's and others, including the Eritreans during their struggle, were all supported and accommodated by the then Somali government. Equally, the Somali opposition groups were assisted by the then Ethiopian regime. For that a psychological briar has been removed, which played a tremendous role for the promotion of social integration as well as inner political emancipation and that is irreversible. For instance, if the Oromas, the most populous ethnic group in Ethiopia and indeed in the Horn were a dormant volcano, they are at present an active volcano and the Tigrians who argue that the Amhara were in a position of power for so long are not prepared to give power so easily. The new Ethiopian constitution recognises certain ethnic rights that were never written before and can be easily invoked." Dr Ahmed added that, "Basically Ethiopia has more problems than Somalia but some powers, specifically the Bush administration and of course Blair of the UK, would like to project otherwise and the reality on the ground is altogether different than the built-up myth."

The view expressed by Somali experts on the Horn and, indeed, in Ethiopia is such that they do not give much weight to the Ethiopian phobia as an anti-Islamic power in the region. Hence, in reality the Muslim populations in Ethiopia are the most numerous in the region and for centuries there have not been religious wars between Somalia and her neighbours.

The prevailing Islamisation of the war on terrorism creates discontent amongst local communities. Much of the conflict in the Horn of Africa has been based on ethnic and clan disputes but not religious confrontations. Furthermore, there has been an existing tradition that promotes harmony between Christian Ethiopians and Muslims in the region. Nonetheless, some of the foreign powers hardly fail in inciting religious difference between the Abyssinian rulers and the Muslims, as the following quotation indicates (from Harvard conference report):

"Shifts in religious affiliation presents a looming danger to Ethiopia. Ethiopia has long been known for its Christian population but, noted one expert, Ethiopia lies on religious fault line. The country's leadership is largely Christian. Christian – Muslim relations in Ethiopia have been fairly peaceful in the last hundred years, but changing religious trends are beginning to challenge the status quo. The Muslim population is nearing parity with Christians and may outnumber them soon due to conversion and higher birth rates. The main Christian population is Ethiopian Orthodox, which is very conservative and not attracting new members, particularly compared to Christian Pentecostal, Evangelical,..".[24.] This kind of statement underpins what the real aims of terrorism combat is all about?

Furthermore, the debate on the degree and the nature of terrorist operatives in Somalia seems evermore present as the following quotations from the Harvard conference mention: "Somalia has played a major role as transit point for terrorism. With its un-patrolled ports, hundreds of unsecured airstrips, and borders with Kenya and Ethiopia, Somalia serves as a trans-shipment point for terrorists. Men, money, material have flowed through Somalia into East Africa for terrorist operations." Another expert said, "Although political Islam is on the rise and terrorists have exploited Somalia's state collapse, these trends have not been as pronounced as might be expected, probably due to the chaotic security environment of a collapsed state".[25] The latter quotation suggests that terrorists would be deterred from finding 'safe haven' in Somalia for the very reasons the first quotation outlined. In other words, if Somalis are not in a position of strength to patrol their borders of sea, air and land, that mystifies the affinity in hosting terrorists. Nonetheless there are terrorists and terrorists. Somalia has been undoubtedly subjected to unspoken 'terrorism'

Many Somalis and non-Somalis argue that, because of the absence of a central state, Somalia has been exploited in multiple forms as follows: Exploitation of Somali territorial waters, illegal fishing, toxic waste dumping, and illegal use of its airspace in so many different forms of air trafficking, including civilian, non-civilian aviation, enigmatic operations and activities in its territorial waters.

It is worth noting the comments made by Ghanim Alnajar, the UN named expert on Somalia during his visit to the Horn region, who remarked that foreign vessels fishing illegally, often armed and in league with local Somali warlords, were taking some $300 million worth of fish each year and that we are talking about a huge robbery that was going on for some time. Alnajar mentioned that the international community neglects Somalia except when it comes to worrying about terrorism. Of particular concern to the world, Alnajar stated, should be rampant abuse of fishing waters of Somalia's long coastline. Mr. Alnajar said that he cannot just sit back and watch and that this has to be highlighted, adding among other things that 'one thing that worries me always is using the pretext of war on terror to harass people.'

It has been reported that some of the US personnel made visits to certain parts of Somali hinterlands. In Mogadishu, in one instance, the community were told by US staff to change the madressas (Islamic schools). Marian Arif, a Somali woman MP replied, "You are asking us to abandon madressas and not helping us to rebuild the destroyed schools. We don't see the madressa the way you described it. On the contrary to your suggestions, young people predominantly get discipline, education and learn respect for elders in the madressa. The majority of the children do not receive proper education since the collapse of the central state, so it is a very small percentage that even gets madressa education. It does not mean one or the other. By and large education is very important for the community development".

The proposition that somehow Somalia is a threat to its neighbours is basically incorrect. Many Somalis hold the view that both Ethiopia and Kenya benefited from Somalia's disarray politically and economically and one may add that both countries learn more about the flourishing culture of Somali entrepreneurship. Substantial numbers of Ethiopians travel to different regions of Somalia for work. The Somalis in Addis-

Ababa contribute to the local economy because of remittances and they were nicknamed 'The god of money' by the Ethiopians. Whilst the Somali refugees in Ethiopia and Kenya are either supported by the UNHCR and others or assisted through family lines, the Ethiopian refugees in Somali territories are not internationally identified and are a burden to the limited resources and work places in the recovered zones of conflict.

In Kenya, the United Nations offices for Somalia have been based in Nairobi since 1991. Jobs have been provided to local Kenyans and there is a large Somali business community that comprises both Somali Kenyans and those from Somalia proper who contribute to the local economy. That has raised the concerns of the Asian community in Kenya, whilst the African Kenyans seem to be picking it up from the Somalis. In addition to that, both Ethiopia and Kenya took part in Somalia's controversial peace negotiations and have seemingly been the most trusted allies in the region against the war on terrorism as the Harvard conference material indicated. For that there have been economic gains of the sort by galvanizing Somali discontent.

In my visit to the Horn in November & December 2006, I did engage substantial research on what Somalis think about the Islamists, the American policy in the region, terrorism issues, the Ethiopian involvement and what one envisages for the future of Somalia and the Somali territories. The views gathered include that it must have been a deliberate attempt to knock Somalia and Somali pride by depriving them of any possible attempt to overcome the endured disarray. That Somaliland was peaceful nobody was forthcoming to recognise. The Islamists brought peace but they are ostracised for that. In the regions of Puntland, despite the fact that they were not pro-secession and were peaceful, no aid for institutional development was forwarded. In the Ogaden region, even though the Addis Ababa government shows the world when famine takes place to attract funds, seldom does assistance reach the Somalis under their jurisdiction. Somalis in the Northern Province of Kenya encounter constant challenge for the resumption of their traditional livelihoods, not by drought, famine and floods, but by reformists and anti-pastoral agencies. On a social level, the spread of qat across Somali speaking territories has risen. The stimulant drug grows in Kenya and Ethiopia and it is marketed mainly for the Somalis. Because of high unemployment and the absence of government regulations, qat has been over-consumed. Both Ethiopia and Kenya were getting substantial amounts of hard currency whilst, from the Somali side, neither of the two countries was exchanging other products. Therefore, from the Somali side, it has not been cost-effective and the drug caused an economic drain to local Somalis. Hence, the only group to discard qat were/are the Islamists. Across the Somali speaking territories the only ones who turned their backs on qat were the Islamists of all ages from young to old. Somalia did not become a Muslim country after the disengagement of the cold war. Somalis have long contributed to Islamic literature and jurisprudence. For example, Imam al-Zayla'i al-Hanafi, from the city of Zayla', produced Tabyin al-Haqa'iq, a well known six volume work used in particular by the Hanafi school of Islamic jurisprudence. His student, Fakhr Abdalla ibn Yusuf ibn Muhammad ibn Ayub ibn Musa al Hanafi al-Zaila'i, also wrote a reference work on Islamic jurisprudence in the 14th century. From the 13th to the 15th century, other Somali literati wrote a number of religious works. Somali teachers and scholars were prominent in Yemen. Dr. Ali Abdi Rahman Hersi wrote more about this subject in unpublished theses. Therefore it is not surprising that the union of the Islamic Courts evoked Islamic jurisprudence when it was most needed.

Moreover, the suggestion that Somalia has been ignored by the international community was disputed. One Somali journalist asserted that Somalia typifies Casablanca in the First World War and, as time passes, the number of agencies whose interests coincide with stateless Somalia grows.

As for the US administration, there is consensus on two points; (1) that the US government under the leadership of the Bush junior is pursuing a policy of revenge against Somalia, thus resuming the intervention where his father Bush the senior left off and (2) that Somalia has been on the list of axis of evil and, since Iraq shackled the US forces, Ethiopia has been subcontracted to do the job on the ground while the US continues to bombard from the air.

With regard to Ethiopia waging war against Somalia, analysts believe that, in the short term, it is obvious that Somalia will lack a regular army of all sorts, aviation as well as other forces, so it has not been well patrolled, and the withdrawal of the Union of Islamic Courts (UIC), for what they called tactical reasons, has curtailed anticipated bloodshed. Nonetheless, in the long term, it may well play against the interest of Prime Minister Meles Zenawi, and of his country. Partly because a disintegrated Somalia through clan lines could be easily united by the faith of Islam, a community that has been classified as 100% Muslims could transcend clanism and the national irredentism could be re-ignited as easily as it was during independence in 1960s. Ethiopian Muslims, who would not have been necessarily unpatriotic if Somalia attacked their country, may not be enthusiastic in waging an aggressive assault against Mogadishu with pre-emptive attacks of a proxy nature. There are also active Ethiopian opposition groups comprised of Somalis, Oromo's and Amharas whose grievance is not faith based but is a nationalistic and territorial endeavour. For that, Ethiopian oppositions of cross-faith argue that, indeed, Meles has a lot of problems at home. So, in many ways, the prime minister of Ethiopia is trying to externalise what is basically a troubled community of his own. Therefore, to understand the perplexities of war-torn Horn of Africa it is important to shed light on Meles Zenawi's political proceedings as the then head of the Tigra Peoples Liberation Front (TPLF) and as the prime minister of present day Ethiopia. In accordance with Ethiopian opposition groups on patriotic gravity, Zenawi does not withstand traditional Ethiopian structure of the Menilik type.

Dr Menbere Asfaw of Ethiopia argues the following in his essay entitled 'who wants to march to war with a traitor?': "...Meles Zenawi...a traitor, once made himself available to the service of Ethiopia's worst enemies including the late Somali dictator Siyad Barre and his former mentor Isaias Afeworki

(Eritrean president). In return to his treacherous service, the Somali dictator …supplied…a diplomatic Somali passport that even the most loyalist Somali was not entitled to. In some of his anti -Ethiopian sermons that he used to preach before he come to power, Meles openly declared that "colonial" Ethiopia occupied and exploited not only Eritrea but also Somali territories including the Ogaden region…the 1977 invasion of Ethiopia by Syaid Barre to annex the Ogaden region was a holy war of liberation…Meles has condemned Emperor Menelik as colonialist for unifying the nation…he is the one who has handed over all our outlets to the sea, making Ethiopia one of the biggest landlocked countries in the world.. He is public enemy number one who has denied the Ethiopian people all their basic freedom…" Dr Menbere Asfaw concluded "…is a Somali Islam or a home-grown tyrant who is threatening the survival of Ethiopia".

International human rights groups including Amnesty International continue to raise concerns about Meles's human rights record. Furthermore, the former U.S. Secretary of State for African Affairs Herman Cohen accused Meles of feeding false intelligence to boost his position. With that entire backdrop and more, Meles has apparently acquiesced alliances with the US and UK wobbly orbit of 'terrorism'. There are three main schools of thought with regard to the grim realities of US involvement on Somalia's internal affairs. The first is those who say that the US would not let Ethiopia occupy Somalia but is in search of erecting a government of its liking, perhaps in the Afghanistan mode. The second school of thought holds the view that it is the American neo-conservatives who are in favour of 'breaking nations' and that the Bush administration negates strong peaceful united Somalia. The third school of thought suggests that the US indeed encourages both Uganda and Ethiopia, who are land-locked, therefore creating more stakeholders in the Horn of Africa and sharpening the anticlimax of Somali Ethiopian animosities.

However in peace, Ethiopia and Somalia could complement each other as good neighbours. Ethiopia can certainly use Somali ports and was using them. On the other hand, populous

Ethiopia could also be a market for Somali entrepreneurship and one should note that there has been a tremendous calming down between the two peoples over the last decade. The architects of Ethiopian invasion to Somali soil failed to consider the long-term consequences of antagonism. On the other hand some argue that indeed Meles himself is in gambling mode, the prime minister of Ethiopia has no aspirations of occupying Somalia territories but he failed to refute against Bush's plan on Somalia and the wider Muslim World.

As for the argument that Ethiopia and the US administration were/are to help the weak TFG (Transitional Federal Government) first of all such an act is very contradictory to the spread of democracy in the region so loudly prescribed by President Bush and Prime Minister Blair. With regard to Meles supporting the US administration against the wishes of many Ethiopians and Somalis that is in effect what the political scientist could call the 'fifth column policy' derived from General Franco of the Spanish Civil War. Franco had an army consisting of four columns and when asked where the fifth column was, he referred to the local supporters inside Madrid. If the Bush administration encourages an arms race in the Horn of Africa that is detrimental to people's lives and it will not go unchecked. The post cold war policy of sending so-called peace keeping or peace enforcement troops to people's lands seems to be nothing less then sovereignty infringement, disruption of local initiative and the undermining of home-based sustainable peace pacts. On the other hand, if sending force to conflict zones is an integral part for peace enhancement around the globe, why don't the United Nations and United States send peace forces to Israel and Palestine?

To sum up, the general viewpoint of most Somalis is that it has been apparent that Somalia has no religious fanaticism. One could argue that there are no organised Islamic based groups per se whose sole aim is to terrorise the world or the west for that matter in Somalia proper, or indeed in any of the Somali speaking territories. Most of the leaders in Muslim countries agree with the anti-terrorism polices.

Traditionally, many Somalis argue that they preferred the then-existing western form of media and freedom of speech in comparison with the then scientific socialism. The Somali brain drain began as early as the 1970's, when many professionals and skilled people resented scientific socialism and the influence of communism. In short, many Somalis sought refuge in the US and the UK. Therefore, people are confused about this new scenario of terrorism and hate and in many ways it does not sink into the population's psyche yet. This questions the degree of its authenticity, as some believe that the US Peace Corps did better public relations for America than is the case with Bush Administration. Therefore, should diplomacy prevail, the US and the UK might have been better off in persuasion than in finger-pointing and muscle-flexing, but if this blanket of Islamic accusation continues, most probably, the confusion and the disproportion created may eventually backfire and that may well be a self-defeating policy.

An Indian scholar who is an economist made the following comment about the relations between economics and the war on 'terrorism': "I tell you one thing, it may be cynicism or call it conspiracy theorist, but this war on terrorism is not convincing and there are a lot of unanswered questions. However, where there are economic competitions, and if someone wants to dominate, to kill or to hamper other financial mechanisms, control of trade roots is one ambition. To put that ambition in practice one has to create a threat, a threat that mobilises your public behind you, at the same time gives one a justification to disrupt international marines and cargo shipment that you don't approve of. This may be where countries like Somalia come in, because of its long coastal line and sharing coastal waters with the Arab world, India plus other Asian countries, taking to an account on the rising market of China and the future market relations between China and the developing world".

It has been indicated that India is in many ways attracting the international world stage of diplomatic politicking. Despite that, however, many Indian thinkers and academicians do promote policies of neutrality and non-alignment. Dr.Premen N. Adddy Indian lecturer on politics and economics from Cambridge at

Ewert House Summertown Oxford stated the following about the US and India relations "A close relations between India and the US does not imply one that is exclusive for India. The latter has fruitful relation with Russia, a legacy of the Soviet period. India has other important relations with other countries including, Japan, china, Egypt indeed countries in Africa and the Latin America and so on. Also India said No to the USA with regard to the coalition against Iraq and had good relations with Saddam Hussein and refused to join the then war against Vietnam. One is aware that the US did Support Pakistan against India when it suited her interest. Hence India discovered the "Green Revolution" that enabled her more self-sufficient on wheat, and is even more confident... Who would prophecies in such a short time India could be one of the ten top countries in technology development...and do not forget that India is a multicultural society "

2 Chapter Two

The Attack on Iraq by the coalition of the willing led by the United States of America on March 2003 has not been taken lightly by the citizens of the world. Indeed politicians may have been reticent but peoples' feelings and concern towards the lost of Iraqi lives, destruction of its infrastructure and looting of Iraqi heritage have been demonstrative cross culturally.

2.1 Iraq: Strangers in the Land of Civilization: The Controversy of the War

As events have unravelled in the United States of America (USA), it has become clearer that President Bush and his team were minded to attack Iraq long before 11/09/01. To put early amnesia at bay, President Bush and Prime Minister Blair told their citizens and the rest of the world that Iraq posed an imminent threat; Saddam Hussein had weapons of mass destruction that would be deployed within 45 minutes to Europe and that he received uranium from Niger, Africa. In the run-up to war, fear was mobilised. As none of the above materialised, the war aims were repackaged into regime change and the liberation and democratisation of Iraq, then grew to sectarian killings and the execution of Saddam Hussein, which George W. Bush expressed as "some kind of revenge killings". What was earlier described as foreign al-Qaida forces destabilising Iraq became labelled as the Sunni terrorists and Shia insurgency.

Bush and Blair never said that Iraq poses a threat because she has high calibre of human resources. Saddam Hussein industrialised Iraq, spent the bulk of national resources inside the country, particularly on education, health and weaponry and Iraq produced high level scientists. The country is rich in water, agriculture, antiquity and oil. Therefore such a combination of resources is simply a threat not only to Israel but also to the American power politics and her stance in global distribution of power. Indeed, Mr. Blair stated in his essay in the Observer newspaper on the 11/4/04, entitled 'why we must never abandon this historic struggle in Iraq': "... the wealth of that potentially rich country, their wealth, their oil..."[26]

On the contrary, the US, the UK and the UN were administering Iraqi oil since the first Gulf War. US deputy defence secretary, Paul Wolfowitz has admitted that oil was the reason for invading Iraq. Speaking to an Asian security Summit in Singapore in June 2003, Wolfowitz said, "let us look at it simply. The most important difference between North Korea and Iraq is that economically we just had no choice in Iraq. The Country is swimming in oil." [27]

Moreover, during the invasion of Iraq, foreign nationals poured into the country like honeybees, whether private contractors (mercenaries) or labour workers hired from Asia, whilst at the same time Iraqi civil servants, technocrats and army forces were mostly tagged as Baathists, unemployment and imprisonment increased,

Sami Ramadani, an Iraqi woman who was a political refugee from Saddam Hussein's regime and is a senior lecturer in sociology at London Metropolitan University, wrote the following in an article entitled "Iraqis told them to go from day one" in the Guardian news paper on 9 April 2004: "Foreign fighters have indeed come flooding into Iraq, not terrorists sent by Bin Laden but mercenaries hired by the occupation authorities. Their role is to carry out dangerous tasks, to help reduce US army casualties. [With] 160,000 occupation forces backed by mass destruction technology... this is in addition to the Pentagon's Israeli-trained special assassination squads. Iraqis now believe that some of the recent assassinations of the scientists and academics were perpetrated by these hit squads. A similar campaign assassination in Vietnam claimed the lives of 41,000 people between 1968 and 1971" [28]

The death toll of Iraqi civilians was estimated at more then 600,000 before the Iraq election. In reality nobody knows the total count as the attacks continued. There are no official statistics. Indeed, during the second assault of Faluja, the British government declined to count the dead. Blair rejects calls for counts of Iraqi dead. The Guardian carried an article on December 9, 2004. Many died in their homes. General Tommy Franks, the US commander in the Iraq war last year [2003] spelt it out before the invasion began. "We don't do body counting...It just is not worth trying to characterise by numbers" Brigadier-General Vince Brooks, the deputy director of operations at US Central Command said just days before the fall of Baghdad: "...And frankly, if we are going to be honourable about our warfare, we are not out there trying to count up bodies. This is not the appropriate way for us to go."[29] There were also the victims of a decade of US/UK/UN imposed sanctions and the oil embargo affair. Some, UN agencies, including FAO and UNESCO commented about the devastating impact of sanctions against Iraqi children: "This figure, generally rounded to 600.000, has been the most frequently cited number." A New York Times article picked up the story and flatly declared: "Iraqi Sanctions Kill Children". In May 1996 CBS-TV's 60 Minutes depicted sanctions as a murderous assault on hundreds of thousands of children ... "UNICEF reported that 4,500 children under the age of five were dying every month in Iraq from hunger and disease." Critics regularly claimed, "More Iraqi children have died as a result of sanctions than combined total of two atomic bombs on Japan and the recent scourge of ethnic cleansing in the former Yugoslavia."[30] Sanctions against Iraq were described as "the most draconian UN embargo in the history of the organisation." When asked whether the UN's sanctions regime was worth the death of 500,000 Iraqi children, Madeleine Albright, then the US ambassador to the UN, replied, "Yes, I think it is worth it."[31]

Not even the Iraqi national heritage was saved. Iraqi libraries and museum treasures have been mainly removed from Baghdad. Some items were immediately targeted and perhaps will be difficult to recover. "...The disappearance of more than 50,000 artefacts from what the Chicago Tribune calls the 'store house of civilisation's cra-Rumsfeld' is far from accident. And it's not like the White House and Pentagon didn't know what was in that storehouse: Leading experts gave them elaborated lists of key artefact sites, placing especial emphasis on the National Museum and artefact sites with objects of ancient civilisation previously described through Biblical chronicles. "Mesopotamia", says Gil Stein, director of the University of Chicago's prestigious Oriental Institute, "is the world's first civilisation. It's first place to develop cities, the first place where writing was invented. And the artefacts from the excavations from there are the patrimony for our entire civilisation and entirely irreplaceable." [32]

According to Khaled Bayomi, a Middle Eastern political researcher who witnessed the looting of the Iraqi National Museum, the American troops inspired the plunder for a very interesting reason; 'The lack of jubilant scenes' of grateful Iraqis greeting American conquerors needed pictures of Iraqis. It is hard to believe that such encouragement did not occur without high-level approval (see US Encouraged Ransacking at www.informationclearing <http://www.informationclearing> house. info/article 2842.ht) [33] Furthermore Donny George, Director of the National Museum of Iraq in Baghdad, told in a packed press conference at the British Museum in London on the 29th of April 04, "The US forces looked the other way while Iraqi museums were being looted. Now they are looking the other way again as many of these looted treasures are taken out of Iraq".

Whilst travelling from Baghdad to Jordan, George encountered some of the looted items in a checkpoint with the American forces and stated: "they are checking every one thoroughly and they have caught a dozen people trying to smuggle looted treasures from Iraqi's museums.... I am very sorry to say that almost all of them have been journalists".[34]

The shrines and the holy places might not have been shipped out, but these historical sites and the relics of Iraq have been also subjected to controversial aerial bombardment, in some cases a battle ground like the Imam Ali shrine in Najaf. Local weddings have been also bombarded. It appeared to be very much an indiscriminate war.

Charles Clover a reporter "embedded" with US troops has this to say in an article in the Financial Times on June 26-27 2004: "Natural-born killers will never win hearts and minds. One of the more jarring memories from my experience covering the war in Iraq …was of young American soldier after a fire-fight in the street of Najaf. During a shootout with a sniper, a blue Fiat raced into the street, trying to escape. The soldier fired 15 rounds from his SAW (Squad Automatic Weapon), killing the driver, who we found out, was an unarmed university professor. An hour later I heard the soldier complaining that his weapon had jammed, preventing him firing off more rounds. Meanwhile, fellow soldiers clustered around him congratulating him on "busting his cherry "-making his first killing …I have always had difficulty understanding how someone like this, an American teenager who probably grew up in some suburb, like me could have this attitude towards taking a life. I saw plenty more like him."[35]

Furthermore, Jonah Goldberg who is a journalist, commented in an article in the Times on 15 may 2004 about the display of the pictures of the Iraqi victims to the war by the media as follows: "Barely two days after the 9/11 attacks, the major news network decided never again to show the images of Americans leaping to their deaths from the World Trade Centre. NBC ran one clip of a man plunging to his death and then admitted it was a mistake. A network vice -president told the New York Times 'Once it was on we decided not to use it again'. …Such restraint is allegedly the norm in the US media. But that norm goes out of the window when there's an opportunity to make America look like barbarian …US media which never reported that FDR in a wheelchair and rarely shows dead American in the TV … But given the opportunity to splash the morning paper with photos of abused Iraqis there was no debate. Show everything they said. Desperate to get in on the story …"[36]

One of the accounts of the Abu Ghraib guard humiliations, published by the Times, May 15, 2004 included "… 870th Military Police Unit who said that the US guards performed voyeuristic sex shows in one out of the way cell, which contained a mattress circled with chairs "for an audience…. the details of the abuse, which were said to have been meted out in an atmosphere of joviality…"[37]

Furthermore, "A Sunday Herald investigation has discovered that coalition forces are holding more than 100 children in jails such as Abu Ghraib ..." UNCIEF was "profoundly disturbed". The Norwegian government, which is part of the coalition of the willing, said "Such assaults are unacceptable. It is against the international laws and it is also unacceptable from a moral point of view..." Ramzi Kysia, an Arab American peace activist, wrote in the Third World Resurgence Magazine in March 2003 "...this is not an accident. It is not a mistake. War is deliberate thing carefully crafted and intentionally executed. And there is a word missing from our lexicon of liberation, "responsibility"[38]

Sami Ramadani, an Iraqi woman lecturer (see above) wrote the following in April 2004: "The US led invasion is daily being unmasked for what it is: a colonialist adventure being met by resistance that will eventually turn in to a an unstoppable war of liberation ...most Iraqis were strongly against the invasion from the start, though it has taken 12 months for the world's media to report that...many Iraqis have decided that the peaceful road to evict the occupiers is not leading anywhere. They do not need Sadr to tell them this. They were told it loudly and brutally...by a US Abraham tank, ...Nor did they fail to notice the article 59 of the new US-engineered constitution, which puts the new US-founded Iraqi armed forces under the command of the occupation forces, which will, in turn, be "invited" to stay in Iraq by the new sovereign government This occupation force will be backed up by 14 large U.S. military bases and the biggest US embassy in the world...."[39] "To be sovereign, theorists said, was to recognise no superior authority and thus to enjoy a plenary discretion over public policy concerning persons and things within the ruler's territory.[40]

The installation of Allawi's government on June 28/04 and the recent elections in Iraq, on January 2005, do not seem to have transformed the situation on the ground. As late as 11 April, 2005 it was reported by the Independent Newspaper that: "The US occupation is as unpopular as ever ...300,000 people demonstrated in the heart of Baghdad on Saturday. Called by the Shia militant leader Muqtada-al-Sadr, it was the largest anti-American demonstration since the overthrow of Saddam

Hussein. Effigies of George Bush, Tony Blair and Saddam Hussein dressed in orange prison jump suits were symbolically thrown down amid cries 'No, No to America! No, No to occupation' Opinion polls confirm that two-thirds of Shia Arabs - 60 percent of Iraqi population - as well as an overwhelming majority of Sunnis want US troops to leave immediately. The Kurds are a fifth of Iraqis, and are the only community fully to support the US."[41] The upsurge of national struggle is unfolding and it seems irreversible.

According to historians, Iraq was never easy to pacify and Iraqis are survivalists. As early as 1258, the Mongols of Asia invaded Muslim countries including Persia and Iraq. At the time the Islamic civilisation was at its peak and so was Iraq. The Mongols were regarded as savages. They destroyed the collected knowledge in the then Iraq. They came with terror and ravaged a richly evolved Muslim civilisation, but at the end most of them converted to Islam and later promoted Islam and elaborated Islamic art and architecture. They turned out to be amongst the best advocates for Islam and the places that they used to ornament with human heads were replaced by finely crafted Islamic arts. Also "In the fourth Umayyad caliph Abdal Malik Ibn Marwan (65/685 to 86/705) dispatched al Hajjaj Ibn Yusuf al Thaqafi the most famous scourge in those times, to subdue a rebellion in Iraq, to teach the inhabitants of Iraq a lesson to respect authorities...."[42] The Iraqis overcame that massacre, as is historically well documented. Furthermore, "after the 1920 revolt (Shia/Sunni unity against the then occupation) ...after killing almost 10,000 Iraqis, the British fundamentally reoriented their strategy in Iraq; they abandoned plans for ambitious nation-building and instead sought a way to transfer power quickly to trustworthy elites..."[43] Could the fate of the occupying forces in Iraq be any different from their predecessors? A Korean proverb says, "It is not necessary to drain the sea to find out if its water is salty."

2.2 Environment

The human and environmental cost of the war against Iraq seems to have been catastrophic and is escalating. The harm that the US led forces inflicted upon the Iraqis and the Iraq landscape is immense. What are even more extraordinary are the magnitude and the duration of warfare in recent day Iraq and how the world seems to be immune to the so-called major assaults waged against Iraqi towns and cities

"As early as January 1991, the US bombardment of the oil facilities in Iraq caused spills of 6 to 8 million barrels of crude oil. A year later that crude oil killed more than 30,000 marine birds. Iraqi water supplies have been poisoned, soil and the plants contaminated and the exposure of the depleted uranium causes cancer and deformity related illnesses".[44]

Furthermore, the US Central Command (CENTCOM) reported that it "used 10,782 cluster munitions, which could contain at least 1.8 million sub munitions. The British used an additional seventy air-launched and 2,100 ground-launched cluster munitions, containing 113,190 sub munitions..." [45] moreover, depleted uranium and the cluster bombs have long-term devastating effects for the local communities. According to experts, the un-exploded bomb continues to kill innocent civilians for years to come and, because of its bright colour, children are most at risk. The health hazard of depleted uranium is enormous. Some Iraqi women are experiencing unusual miscarriages and some children are born with deformities, including head enlargement.

After the Fallujah massacre, Dr Salam Ismael, who returned to Fallujah, where he worked as a doctor, cited the following: "It was the smell that first hit me, a smell that is difficult to describe, and one that will never leave me. It was the smell of death. Hundreds of corpses were decomposing in the houses, gardens and streets of Fallujah. Bodies were rotting where they have fallen - bodies of men, women and children, many half eaten by wild dogs. You may think you know what happened in Fallujah but the truth is worse then you could possibly have imagined…"[46]

The question is how this could go down well in the consciences of those who are responsible in authorising and sustaining the war in Iraq, especially when Prime Minster Blair made public his claim on Christian-value morals. The Archbishop of Canterbury, in an interview, published by the Observer newspaper on July 11, 2004 about Tony Blair, war and God, said the following: "Anyone making decisions involving the lives of others must answer to God". He added: "In life, Tony Blair and George W. Bush might have to live with the knowledge that the death and the destruction in the Iraq war could not morally be justifiable."[47]

Europe lost 15 million, mostly soldiers, in World War I and at least 41 million in World War II, mostly civilians"[48]. In the light of that, one would think that the lessening of the appetite for war would be extended to the wider world.

.

2.3 The Kurdish factor and how the Baathist came to power

When the Ottoman Empire collapsed and the British army then led by general Sir Stanley Maude invaded Baghdad in 1917 during the First World War, the people in Iraq were led to believe that the British were to liberate them but not to conquer. In November 1918 the Anglo-French declaration was issued. Their goal, they proclaimed "was the complete and final liberation of the peoples who have for so long been oppressed by the Turks, and the setting up of national governments and administrations that shall derive their authority from the free exercise of the initiative and choice of the indigenous people"[49] Whilst that was the public declaration, in private the colonial powers were partitioning the territories under the Ottoman Empire among themselves. Shortly after the declaration, the Kurdish leader Sheikh Mahmud Al- Hafeed, who kept a copy of the declaration and believed the British explanation, set up a national government and a state for the Kurdish people in the Kurdish territories of the north, but that hope was short-lived. In May

1919 British troops destroyed the Kurdish state. The Kurds continued to resist the British policies towards them and the Kurdish revolts against the British had a tremendous impact on the British occupation in Iraq. Nevertheless, as one American historian explained, "… both in Iraq and Iran this served among other purposes…. To keep the Kurdish question as a tactical reserve in case of difficulties with Baghdad or Tehran".[50] The Kurdish aspirations for self-determination continued to be entertained. This was echoed during the first Gulf War and again while Bush and Blair were evoking Saddam Hussein's brutality against the Kurdish people and emphasising the plight of the Kurdish people. In practice, the reality was different as the following quotation indicates: "British pilots protested in 2001 at being ordered to return to their base in Turkey to allow the Turkish air force to bomb Kurds. The Washington Post reported, "On more than one occasion [US pilots] have received a radio message that there is Turkish Special Mission (TSM) heading to Iraq". The US pilots were then required to return to base. When the pilots flew back into Iraqi airspace they would see 'burning villages, lots of smoke and fire'…"[51]

These kinds of contradictions might also have an impact on the minds of the decent service men and women in the army. It is no wonder that there have been reports of suicides, nervous breakdowns and nightmares amongst some of the American and British troops in Iraq. It has been reported by Human Rights Watch that "over 600 members of the US army serving in Iraq have been flown home of (sic) psychiatric reasons since the country was invaded in March 2003, and the number keeps rising so long as the occupation of Iraq continues. Furthermore, US army medical staff believes up to 20% of American military personnel will suffer from post-traumatic-stress disorder and some committed suicide"[52] The more the occupation continues, the more the casualties of psychiatric illnesses increase.

The Lebanese say, "There is not a tree which the wind cannot shake". According to a young American soldier interviewed by Channel Four news London, he believed that there are voices in his head that tell him you are "suicidal homicidal". He said that 60% of the US forces in Iraq are under drugs because of the war in Iraq and many expressed that what they were told by the authorities and the reality on the ground is quite different.

2.4 How the Sunni and the Baathist came to power

In 1920, Najaf in Iraq was the centre of the then Shiite and Sunni revolt against the British occupation. However the Shia and the Sunnis overcame their differences and united for the struggle and the liberation of Iraq against the British occupation. The Ulama Al Diin (Religious Scientists) mobilised the Iraqi people. The Sunni and Shiites celebrated together and attended each other's events and ceremonies. The resistance grew and gained momentum. One Iraq Sunni put it in a poem, "O you the people of Iraq, you are not orphans to seek guardianship [a mandate] for Iraq. You shall no longer enjoy the water of Tigris if you content with humiliation and oppression"[53]

The British found it impossible to crush and subsequently used weapons of mass destruction against the Iraqi people; a poison gas as they call it. "The British imported Faisal Hussein, the son of Sharif Hussein of Mecca…and arranged for him to become the king of Iraq…together with a small urban group and powerful tribal leaders from the country-side, constituted the foundation of what was to become an overwhelmingly Sunni dominated state."[54] The majority of the Sunnis were in the Ottoman army and were generally more educated. Furthermore, Faisal was acceptable by the majority of the Shiites because he was Ahal al-Beit (from the Prophet's lineage).

As early as July 1958, Iraqi Brigadier Abd al-Karim al-Qasim and the free officers' movement challenged the monarchy and the colonial political status quo. However, the most well established Iraqi political party was the Iraqi communist party (ICP) that was founded in 1934. The party was reputable for its tenacity as well as its struggles. In the 1940's and 1950's their membership expanded, which they mainly drew from the Shiite and they extended a helping hand to Brigadier Qasim. The other Iraqi major political party was the Baath Party predominantly Sunni and was established much later then the ICP. The Baathists made an attempt to overthrow Qasim (Saddam Hussein was a participating member). That was not successful and, as a result, many of the Baathist leaders fled the country. The Baathists were against the communists and in many ways considered themselves as nationalist. The Americans were worried about the spread of communism in the region. In 1959, the then CIA director, Allen Dulles, had already described Iraq as 'one of the most dangerous places on earth'. The CIA started to establish contacts with the exiled Baathist leaders to work out plans for the overthrow of Qasim. In the 17-30 July 1968 revolution in Iraq by the Baath party, whilst the leadership of the party were preparing for their activities to overthrow the then Iraq regime, it surprised them to learn that the general director of the military intelligence director Abdul Rasaq al Naif, knew all their activities. He then threatened them (Baathists) to disclose their plans to the regime should they not accommodate his propositions. That meant they would suffer more in the hands of the then regime. Thus the leadership of the Baath party agreed with the director to take part in the revolution. Consequently, Abdul Rasaq al Naïf became the prime minister while leader of the party became the president. This situation was unacceptable to many members of the Baathist party who thought that their revolution would be accused of being an American coup d'etat, since its prime minister was well known as the US man in Iraq. Thus the Baathist party, on 30th of July 1968, got rid of the prime minister and his close friend, Ibrahim al-Dawasd, who was the minister of defence and both of them were appointed as ambassadors in Europe. However, from the US part, according to this quotation: "The plan to overthrow the Iraq leader, [was} led by William Lakeland who was stationed at Baghdad embassy… [Even then] … the agency was instrumental in supplying the names of the communists to be eliminated… some of which were taken from their homes and murdered"[55]. While Baathist went on to govern, the Egyptian journalist Hassanein Heikl published many of these interviews with leaders in the region.

Therefore, the present day US/UK policy against Iraq with regard to the emphasis put on local grievances of the Shiites, Sunni and Kurds has been consistent with that of the earlier interventions. The US is not a homogenous society, so it need not be an issue for multi-ethnic Iraq. Many Iraqis argued that there is no distinct separation of the sort with regard to the ethnic division on Shiite majorities, Sunni Arabs or Kurds because there are Shiite Arabs, Sunni Kurds, and Arab Christians. There are also the cross ethnic groups of secularists vis-à-vis religious groups. So it is not as simplistic as the media led us to believe.

It is worth noting that throughout history, intermarriage between the Iraqi communities has been common and therefore many are related to one another.

The closure of Muqtada al-Sadr′s newspaper and repression of Al Jazeera television does not stand for the liberty and democracy that one is told to be one of the core reasons for the invasion of Iraq.

3. Chapter Three

Despite the fact that some of the western media as well as the film industry continued passing judgments on Islam and the Arab world never before have we witnessed the type of attack that have been unleashed since 9/11/2001. This chapter therefore aims to explore the degree of hate apparatus and the paradigms of fear in the context of the new war of terrorism vis-à-vis occupation.

3.1 Who hates whom?

In the ensuing battle of fear and hate matters, the leaders of the coalition of the willing as well as their counterparts in Israel often state that those who hate them are, "a threat to democracy and are against western values". Such words become the norm in most of their speeches, not to mention the constant reference to "terrorism". The Israeli government in particular dismisses almost anybody who says the injustice against the Palestinians as anti-Semitic. But views in the Arab world and the wider Muslim world are different. People believe that they are not in a position of hate and indeed they are not only forgiving but they also remain hospitable regardless. That does not mean they forget the miscarriages of justice and the inherited colonial legacies because boundary demarcations continue to affect people's lives. When the British occupied most of the lands that were then under Ottoman rule, promises were made but were not kept. More so, the creation of the state of Israel that manifested itself in the demolishing of Palestinian villages and changing their names has not been taken lightly by the victims. Therefore, there is abundant knowledge among people on what went wrong, when and how. Stories are narrated and passed from one generation to another and it does not need an expert to explain.

An Arab woman who is head of the women's NGO in Cairo, Egypt was interviewed about what she thinks of anti-Israeli or Jewish sentiments in the Arab world and she replied the following:

"It is not that we Arabs began to hate the Jews in one day. We are not anti-Semitic. Indeed we are Semites too. The real issue is a territorial dispute as well as the occupation of Palestine culminated by a continuation of injustices, deception and the likes... it is also important to stress that there is no holy war, or Islam against Christianity or Judaism. Islam might be a unifying factor for beleaguered communities."

Also, a woman lawyer in Cairo was asked about the issue of fear and she replied the following:
"There is a fear and there is a fear. At this end we do not believe that we are in fear, but we are angry and frustrated. Every wrongdoing in the western and Israeli book of modern politics has been practised on us. Thus our national pride has been tarnished. The real fear, or rather insecurity that needs to be addressed is the self-inflicted type in the context of misuse and abuse of power; a power in which one fears to lose and fears about the future. Such a climate of insecurity and general anxiety, such a state of mind is dangerous to world peace by and large."

Nuala Young, previously lecturer on European cultures at Oxford Brooks University, states the following on the issue of anti-Semitism with regard to European views: "First of all nobody has explored the motives behind the persecution of the Jewish people. They just allowed a sense of unease to have developed around the issue, such that nobody will discuss it. Each of the countries in Europe has a different history of collaboration with the persecution. For instance about 80% of Jews in Holland were deported to concentration camps, whereas, in Denmark, about 90% of Jews were saved. Particularly in France there was a hidden scar of resentment between those who collaborated and those who had resisted. So now we have situation in Europe where, because of what is happening in Israel and Palestine liberal people are critical of the Israeli government but are scared to be accused of anti-Semitism. At the same time you have the old undercurrent of the original anti-Semitism still lingering in those European countries."

However, in the Arab world, there was no persecution of the Jews. Quite the contrary, it was the heyday of the Islamic civilisation in Andalusia that Jewish people refer to as the golden age since they benefited from it. "...as citizens of the Islamic State, the Jew could model his life after the Torah and do so legitimately, supported by the public laws of the state where he resided. For the first time, a non–Jewish state put its executive power at the service of a rabbinic court. For the first time, the state- institution assumed responsibility for the maintenance of Jewishness, and declared it ready to use its power to defend the Jewishness of Jews against the enemies of Jewishness, be they Jews or non-Jews. After centuries of Greek, Roman and Byzantine (Christian) oppression and persecution, the Jews of the Near East, of North Africa, of Spain and Persia looked upon the Islamic state as liberator. Many of them readily helped its armies in their conquests cooperated enthusiastically with the Islamic state administration. This cooperation was followed by acculturation into Arabic and Islamic culture, and produced a dazzling blossoming of Jewish arts, letters, sciences and medicine. It brought affluence and prestige to the Jews...Indeed Judaism and its Hebrew language developed their 'golden age' under aegis of Islam. Hebrew acquired its first grammar, the Torah its jurisprudence ...Judaism developed its first mystical thinker as well...".[56] basically, the recognition of the Torah is an Islamic principle. It was during the establishment of the state of Israel that Arabs were antagonised and obviously since then not much love is lost between them.

The view of the Arab public is that, by and large, the UK created the state of Israel. The US endorsed it, and continued to support it. As one American protestant put it, "We are using them {Israel} and they are using us." With regard to Arab states, some of them established diplomatic and commercial relations with Israel. In particular Israel has embassies in Egypt, Jordan and commercial links with Oman and Qatar. The American and European Jews are knowingly allowed to engage their jobs and business in the Arab countries. So to normalise Arab Israeli relations depends a lot on Israeli leaders' policies in the region and more so in Palestine. The Arabs managed to come to terms with injustices against the Palestinian people. Not only do they recognise Israel's right to exist, but the Palestinians also accept the almost unthinkable land compromises for their own country and settlements suggested in Madrid, Oslo, Copenhagen and other peace accords that have, however, failed to materialise.

One British/Israeli Jew, Dr. Stephen Fulder, trains peace activists said the following: " The hard fact is the Arabs do not hate us as much as our government wants us to believe, and they have plenty reasons to hate us. The Eastern European Jews are the worst with regard to Palestinian rights…"

Judy Lown, an Israeli social worker, also mentioned that, "until 1948 there were no Israelis but there were Canaanites and Israelites and at present there is an organisation called 'Children of Abraham" in Israel that encourages peace between Palestinians and Israelis, not to mention Jews".

However, most aspects of the religious history are commonly shared. Judaism is the first religion believing in one God and the Muslims inherit many of its tenets. The Arabs are also children of Abraham. After Abraham, many nations were replaced whilst others integrated. The devolved nations and actors in the region included the people of Pharaoh, who were not Arabs but African Cushities, the Phoenicians, Sumerians, the Persians, and others. It is generally believed that the Israelites were part of that pool of historical dynamics of different perspectives in different times. In short, the present day conflict is based on Israel's occupation of Palestine and other captured Arab lands including the Golan Heights of Syria and Israel controls the waters of the occupied landscape. Thus it should be addressed and dealt with accordingly. There is no real Judaic/Islamic discourse at present or in contemporary history and it would be unwise to go along that road.

Many observers of the Middle East conflict note that, since the Nasirites of Egypt, the Arabs have been in many ways politically docile. But the more the recent administrations of Israel and the US capitalise on their weakness, the more they should be exposed to international scrutiny. So far, Arabs have continued to have relationships with the UK and US irrespective of their historical records and the fact that the US continues to block the UN resolutions in support of Palestinian rights. The Arabs, particularly the oil-producing countries, share their wealth with the world. They have invested in the west. They contributed to the development of western financial institutions. The US has military bases in most parts of the region. The British have their main base in Oman.

The Arabs contributed to the first Gulf war in many ways, with little exception. The Iraqis are paying the cost of the very war that devastated them. Kuwait, Bahrain and Qatar provided military bases for the coalition. The preference for British and American expatriates in the region has been common. Moreover, when the US and UK were at odds with Iran, the rest of the Arab League tuned in and were supportive of the west. The Saudis extended a helping hand to the US against the then Soviet Union in Afghanistan, Somalia and Yemen.

With regard to the war against terrorism, the Arab governments are in line with US/UK prescriptions. So who hates whom? As a Somali would say, "If you have your hand on the she camel's hump, you need not to stretch higher by wanting more, you may otherwise lose it all."

Alistair Cooke, former British intelligence officer who worked in the Middle East among other places, wrote the following in an article in the Guardian on December 10, 2004: "We must realise [that] Muslims don't hate our values - they hate our policies. The rhetoric that we in the west are engaged in a "war on terrorism" is so embedded in our thinking that most accept the phrase without question ... One piece of evidence often cited by "terrorist experts" for the war on terror is the existence of "terrorist training camps" in Afghanistan, Yemen and Bekaa Valley of Lebanon. But these were not terrorist training facilities at all. I knew these camps for 20 years...they were trained to fight an insurgence against western forces and against pro-western regimes. ."[57] Sir Ivor Roberts, British Ambassador to Italy, also reported to believe that President George Bush is the "greatest recruiting sergeant for al-Qaida" was speaking off the record when he expressed this view at a conference in Tuscany. According to the Italian newspaper Corriere Della Sera, "The statement itself is hardly original ...[but] provides powerful evidence that some senior civil servants were opposed to Tony Blair's unqualified backing for Mr. Bush's war strategy … John Kerry, [the then] Democratic presidential candidate also disagreed with this … accusing his Republican rival of "colossal" errors of judgment and diverting resources from the war on terriorism"[58] Furthermore, according to the following quotation, US intelligence and military sources said: "The Israeli Defence Force {IDF} has sent urban warfare specialist to Fort Bragg in North Carolina; the home of US Special Forces…Israeli military "consultants" have also visited Iraq…"[59]

It is also worth noting that Israel made attacks against Iraqi military facilities unilaterally just to hamper Iraqi's weaponry capabilities during Saddam Hussein's regime. Israel allied with France and UK during the Suez crisis and the three attacked Egypt in 1956 when Egypt attempted to nationalise the Suez Canal. With regard to the wider Muslim world, Israel also threatens Iran and Pakistan every so often. Israel supported and provided military equipment and expertise to Ethiopia against Somalia during the 1977/78 Horn of African Conflict. Furthermore, some Israeli authorities as well as a substantial number of Jewish journalists have exhibited outright antagonism against Muslims in media assaults in the west. Certainly one of the examples that outrage the bulk of the Muslim world is the Israeli idea of welcoming any European, African or Asian Jew whilst the Palestinians are not allowed to exercise the right to return to their homelands and they remain as refugees in camps.

There is a catalogue of injustice. A set of questions arises about the symptoms and the causes as well as animosities and inequities. This current phenomenon of "hate" syndrome is not only enigmatic, but an obstacle to dialogue and it needs to be addressed. There is a Somali saying that explains: Hasha geela cunta ee cabaada. (The she camel that bites the camels yet screams for help).

In terms of civilities, respect versus segregating, antipathy and religious hate, it is worth quoting Yvonne Ridley, who is a British woman journalist converted to Islam after having been exposed to the Taliban in Afghanistan as a reporter. She wrote the following in an article in the Observer on 12 December 2004, P27: "Wearing a head scarf is not a big deal...unless you happen to be a Muslim, ...When I converted to Islam I knew I would have to embrace the Muslim headdress. As for many converts, it was a huge stumbling block...when I finally did, the repercussions were enormous ... from that moment I became a second-class citizen ... I knew I would become a target for abuse from the old Islam-phobic oik, but I did not expect so much open hostilities from complete strangers..." One journalist friend commented "I am worried that this anti-Islamic sentiment may spread like the then anti-Semitism." One English Professor also stated that "hence the defeat of the USSR what will be the next target bombing Muslims." Against that backdrop the questions that arise include: Why does one need an enemy? Is it a pathological hype to energise aggression and how can one proclaim civilities, morals and decent values when one wages wars of indiscriminate nature? On the other hand, how can one demand normalisation and respect when one provides aggression and broken promises? There are more discussions of the sort in the following chapters.

3.2 The partition and the occupation of Palestine

The Middle Eastern religious fixation (the connections between beliefs, places, identities, in the context of Israeli Palestinian dispute) is one of those issues where past and present are crucially interconnected. Therefore, to understand the present-day conflict in the region, it is important to reflect on some historical background. It is worth noting that, "for three centuries before Jesus, Palestine and the whole Near Eastern world was flooded by Hellenism; an ideology and worldview deriving from the older roots of Egyptian religion as well as the reaction of provinces against Greek and Roman naturalism."[60] In more modern times, Palestine was under Turkish rule from 1516 until the fall of the Ottoman Empire at the end of the First World War. "Then Palestine was conquered by Britain. Anxious for Jewish support, the British foreign secretary, Arthur Balfour, pledged British support for the Zionists in making Palestine a national home for the Jewish people. But the pledge contradicted one given to the Arabs, who thought that Palestine was to become an independent Arab state after the war. When the war ended, the British, in fact, continued to rule Palestine under a League of Nations mandate…The British then proposed to divide the country between the two groups."[61]

"The Zionist movement was founded by the Hungarian Jew Theodore Herzl to press for the restoration of Palestine to the Jews. This movement grew rapidly, and increase numbers of European Jews began to immigrate to Palestine. Financial aid came from American Zionist, as well as British Jews…"[62]

Consequently, as a result of the document known as the Balfour Declaration, on May 14 1948, the independent state of Israel was proclaimed. The UN in 1947 proposed that Palestine be divided into Jewish and Arab states with Jerusalem in the middle for both to share. The Arabs rejected the plan from day one and the Arab-Israel conflict started as early as 1948. Shortly afterwards, Palestinians were displaced from their own lands and homes, thus becoming refugees. In the words of the Israeli historian, Avi Shlaim, "The result of a Jewish Military Offensive designed to clear the interior of the future Israeli State and involved the forcible expulsion of Arab civilians."[63]

The most notable wars between the Arabs and the Israelis include the 1967 six day war, in which Egypt attempted to regain the land she lost in 1956 and blocked the Gulf of Aqaba. That move resulted in Israel capturing more land, including Sinai of Egypt, the Golan heights of Syria, the west Bank of the Jordan, the Gaza Strip and East Jerusalem. This brought the Palestinian refugees under the military control of the Israelis. As a result, the Israelis built "settlements" all across the military occupied territories. They also encouraged more Jewish immigrants with an incentive to settle the occupying territories. The Palestinians bitterly resisted this occupation. As they say in Mogadishu "no enemy is too small and no animosity should be belittled".

On the 6th of October 1973, the Arabs, in particular Egypt and Syria, waged a surprise attack against Israel, mainly to regain their territories. It was the first of its kind, known as the Yom

Kippur War by the Jews and the Ramadhan War by the Arabs; "a war that proved the costliest and potentially the most dangerous of the four that Israel had fought in the generation since it was founded." [64] The Arabs got their territories back until the intervention of the US. On the whole it was the US pilots and the American intervention in the war that enabled Israel to regain sovereignty and to continue occupying more Arabs lands.

President Anwar Sadat of Egypt stated in one of his speeches, "I have proven that we can defeat Israel without the US involvement of the war ...but we cannot defeat the super power."

Sadat, became a pragmatist, pursuing a policy of détente and then established diplomatic relations with Israel. That enabled Egypt to regain Sinai, but has damaged Arab solidarity ever since. Furthermore a number of AU (African Union) countries that were previously in support of Egypt opened diplomatic relations with Israel since Egypt entered peace with Israel.

Israel also welcomed Sadat's diplomatic move, as she was keen on the issue of normalisation with her neighbours. An Israel commentator stated, "Saddat defeated us twice, once in war and the other in peace," referring to when Sadat, made the unilateral decision to enter peace with Israel and that he had been the first Arab leader to visit Tel-Aviv.

Therefore, given the historical conditions of the current Arab-Israeli conflict, it is evident that the conflict is ultimately related to the people's deepest aspirations for freedom and human rights, including economics and social development. It is a matter of occupation vis-à-vis. struggle for liberation. Therefore, it is of paramount importance to distinguish the Palestinian national cause from religious fundamentalism and the 'hate factor! Although the majority of Palestinians adhere to Islam, the most radical Palestinian, who opposed any Arab concessions to Israel because Israel was not ready to reciprocate, was a Christian born Palestinian, Dr George Habash. He was born into a Greek Orthodox family who were forced to leave their home in Lydda, Palestine in July 1948. Dr Habash was the founder of the Arab National Movement as well as the Popular Front for the

Liberation of Palestine, the then leading Palestinian Marxist party. He once said, "If we cannot obtain our rights through international legality then revolutionary legality is the solution". In an interview with Al-Ahram weekly in Egypt, on what he thought of the peace process, he said the following: "The collapse of the Soviet Union and the disintegration of the Arab order have had a negative impact on the Arab liberation movement. The United States and Israel saw this as a chance to impose their hegemony and thus implement the Israeli project. From here came the idea they call the 'Peace Processes'. In fact, it is total hegemony over the region. They want to implant the Zionist project in Palestine; they want to prove to the whole world that Israel's presence is legal in the full meaning of the word."[65]

Dr Habash's group, (PLF Palestinian Liberation Front) were famous in the hijacking of the three planes at Sarqa airport in 1970 that unleashed the event known as Black September.

Other leading Palestinian diplomats' academics and politicians who rigorously advocate the Palestinian causes were also born in Palestinian and from Christian families. Among them is Dr Hanan Ashrawi, a Palestinian woman, who upstaged Netanyahu (former Israel Prime minister) at a peace conference in Madrid. The US ABC news describes her as a person who, "masterfully conducts press conferences and interviews, controls the topics of discussion, dodging uncomfortable issues and cutting what she considers irrelevant questions." She was very successful in presenting the more realistic image of the Palestinian people not as terrorists but as oppressed people."[66]

Professor Edward Said, then in Colombia, University, the author of many books including 'Blaming the Victims', 'The end of the peace, Gaza to Jericho', 'Orientalism' that was translated to 36 languages including Hebrew, was born into a Christian Palestinian family and spent most of his life advocating the Palestinian cause. Friends and foes admired him. Other examples include the Palestinian ambassadresses, to Jordan Layla Khalid, to France Leila Shahed and the Palestinian representative in London, Afif Safia. Therefore, what is most disturbing is not only to disguise the Palestinian plight as Islamic jihadist, but also to lump it with the new war of terrorism and the Al-Qaida mystic, of the post cold war phenomenon!

In the western controlled media and in particular the UK and the US, this conflict is usually reported as if it were a war of equals. Also, the Jewish and Israeli peace activists seldom are given publicity. Even the views of decent Israelis and Jews who do not agree with Prime Minister Sharon's polices against the Palestinians have not been given enough coverage. A British Jewish Woman in Oxford, at a cross-faith peace march in Oxford against the Iraq war that was addressed by Rabbi, Bishop and Imam, said that her brother who is a doctor and peace activist finds it very difficult to make his views heard.

Edward Kessler, director of the Centre for Jewish-Christian Relations, Cambridge wrote the following in the Independent newspaper: "...Today in Israel military force and violence are being used aggressively as well as defensively, for conquest as well as for self-defence. The government of Israel has chosen the path of the Gentile nations by building tanks, aircraft and bombs, and now fences and walls...this reversion to the Biblical path leads to a dead-end. And I do mean a dead end". Mr. Kessler continued, "One Israeli leader opposing Ariel Sharon's policy is Avraham Burg, who was Speaker of Knesset from 1999-2003. He has also acknowledged the dead-end towards which Israel is moving. Burg has courageously called for a change of course. There is not much time, he warns. The time for decision has arrived.... We love the entire land of our forefathers and in some other time we would have wanted to live here alone but that will not happen. The Arabs too have dreams and needs. Burg calls on Diaspora Jews, for whom Israel is one pillar of their identity, to be bold and speak out."[67] Furthermore, some Israeli pilots also refused to carry out assassination missions that would kill more innocent Palestinians. One Israeli pilot told a journalist in an interview for Channel Four Television (London based television station) that the Palestinians have nothing but desperation, and that the Israeli military is well equipped and that there is no need for heavy-handedness.

In addition to the above, Tali Fahima, a 29 year old Israeli who voted for Ariel Sharon and believes that Israel is struggling for survival against terrorism, decided to meet Zakariya Zubeidi, a Palestinian who has been described as the Jenin leader of the al-Aqsa Martyrs Brigade responsible for suicide bombing in Israel. Ms. Fahima decided that she would ask Mr. Zubeidi why he killed Jews. When she met him and had several more meetings Fahima, described him as a freedom fighter "and a kind-hearted person whom I was lucky to meet". She become a peace activist and told the Jerusalem Post the following: "Who causes the occupation? The Palestinians? No. It is the Israelis and who am I? A Jew and an Israeli and by sitting at home and doing nothing I am also responsible...Zubeid is not a terrorist, he is fighting against the occupation. Suicide bombers are also fighting the occupation. Put yourself in their place and see what happens. They are denied basic rights and freedom". [68] When detained by the Israeli authorities, Fahima's friend Lin Dovrat stated the following: "They tried to kill Zubeidi five times and failed and she ...was able to connect with him on very basic human level and I think that drives them nuts."[69]

On August 28, 2004, the Guardian newspaper published a piece entitled 'The Palestinians want an end to their Solitary Confinement' that explained the following: " ... Israeli troops ran amok in the camps, making mass arrests, beating women and children, shooting civilians at will and adding to the huge prison population currently well over 7,500. According to Israeli sources, more then 650,000 Palestinian men and boys have gone through Israeli detentions at some point in their lives..." [70]

It has been reported that, " Ariel Sharon's chief aide claimed that the real purpose of the Israeli prime minister's disengagement plan was to freeze the peace and prevent the establishment of a Palestinian state, all with the blessing of the US. Dov Weisglass, Mr. Sharon's chief of staff and the man appointed as representative in negotiations with the White House, boasted that he had won an agreement from the Americans for Israel to keep almost all Jewish settlers in the West Bank"[71]

Moreover, whilst it has been obvious that the US is neither a neutral body nor an honest broker in the Palestinian-Israeli conflict, countries with no vested interest need to be encouraged for mediation and reconciliation. It is such situations that provoke one to ask whose world it is!

To sum up, the evidence, presented in previous pages suggests that there hasn't been much of a change in the history of dividing, sub-dividing and re-dividing the Iraqi community. The British were preferential to the Sunnis against the majority Shiites during the colonial period, the United States supported the Baathists and allied with Saddam Hussein against Iran and Iraqi opposition groups and both internal and external protagonists have failed to do justice for the Kurdish people. In short, the policy of widening the gap of sectarianism in Iraq has not been changed; only positions have been swapped.

The war against Iraq exhibits the dichotomy between the traditional concept of "sovereignty" and contentious legalisation of interventionism in the name of democratisation. It also engages doubts on claiming liberation for Iraq whilst civilians are not spared abuse and torture. Hence the awareness of the illegality of the war against Iraq is gaining momentum. The matters of the absence of weapons of mass destruction and the dynamics of misleading the public have been revealed as time progresses.

In the light of all that, the challenge that western democracy, in particular that of the US and UK, faces is what measures should be undertaken in terms of accountability at human, economic and infrastructure levels for the catastrophic war on Iraq. On the whole, international legal obligations, morality, humanity and the significance of precedence action should not be a one-way street.

The other most challenging issues include authority versus participation, demonising of leaders and collective punishment (i.e. failure to separate the leader from the nation or the people), in other words, the preparedness to invade and to destroy a nation's wealth and infrastructure in the name of one man. How is this different from the piratical traditions of earlier times? And how far has civilisation evolved in the passage of time? In the final analysis, the war against Iraq might have displayed the worst scenarios in modern warfare, in which theoretical principals fail to match practices. The leaders of the coalition of the willing seem to have dubious relationship with the truth. Mr. Blair says, "We will stay until the job is done, and whatever necessary it takes".

A Somali proverb says *"waan baahan-ahay bahktiga looma cuno.* " Do not eat carrion even if you are hungry". In other words, do not bring shame upon you in any circumstances.

As for Palestine, strictly speaking the case in question is one of occupation. The Palestinian struggle is neither jihadist based nor terrorist marked and it is not a territorial dispute either. Indeed, when most of the former British colonies, protectorates and mandates were achieving independence, Palestine was scrambled and the state of Israel was formed. The rest is history. The Palestinian people are therefore yearning for what most of us take for granted, which is freedom and respect. It is very simple to understand and of all people on this planet it is the Jewish people who must know better. Every time the Palestinian people exercise their right to choose their leaders, those leaders are criticised as weak, jihadist, terrorist or all three. Therefore demonising and dodging Palestinian endeavour through the modern media cannot mask the facts about Palestine and the horrendous occupation.

4. Chapter Four

It is worth noting how the present day war tactics of President Bush seem to be consistent with the historical pattern of imperial adventure including the medieval wars during the early centuries of Byzantium. We may also reflect briefly on how the west in general, the US and UK in particular continue to fail to acknowledge adequately what they owe to the Islamic and Middle Eastern civilisations. Therefore, whilst evidence in the previous pages presents issues on the ground and inherited colonial legacies, scepticism about the arguments of terrorism, Iraqi weapons of mass destruction and the democratisation factor need to be tackled.

4.1 The terrorism factor and testimonies!

For instance, on the issue of terrorism, many argue that the threat from terrorism has been inadvertently exaggerated. It has been reported, "Germany is to drop September 11 plot charges because evidence against the only man jailed for terrorism attack is so weak".[72] Moreover, Lotfi Raissi, an Algerian pilot who was arrested in Britain in September 2001 for a false allegation of training the September 11 hijackers, was later released in February 2002 when a judge ruled that there was "no evidence to suggest he was connected to 9/11 or any form of terrorism." The Times in London on October 11, 2006 carried an article about Mr. Raissi, entitled, "Not a shred of evidence pilot was part of 9/11," by Sean O'Neill. Lofti Raissi is said to protest against the damage to his reputation and loss of career as a pilot.

In the UK, a report published by the institution of race relations on 3rd September 2004 that examined all arrests made since september/11/2001 mentioned that "...most of those convicted under anti-terrorist laws in the last three years are non Muslims despite the publicity of Muslim arrests." For instance, out of the 609 Muslims that were arrested, 15 were tried and of those 15, only three were convicted. Subsequently, two of them have been granted leave to appeal. The author of the report, Dr Harmil Athwall added the following "...that reflects the institutionalisation of anti-Muslim racism in police operations and the criminalisation of entire communities" [73].

The Mayor of London Ken Livingstone, had this to say about the British government's new anti terror laws on March 13, 2005, "Tony Blair's argument that the threat from Osama Bin Laden justified the introduction of control orders was ridiculous …the terror threat was now less then during the IRA's heyday…my big worry about the legislation is you rely on the advice of the security service. The danger comes from two or three disaffected men doing something more like a car bomb. We are more at risk of dying from bird flu than we are from being blown up by any terrorist… " [74] However, since the 7th and 21st of July 2005 bomb attacks in London, a lot has changed in the UK. Despite the fact that the general consensus appeared to be that the terrorist threat is no longer speculative, but real, the existing gaps between terrorism threats and reality have not been narrowed

The story that an Egyptian scientist masterminded the July 7th bomb attacks in London was dropped as he gave an official interview and his name was cleared. In connection with the failed July 21st bombings, the initial belief that most of them were Somalis has been incorrect. The Italian interior minister stated that the Somalis do not have this culture or types of attacks and that the British should look more closely to people who sought asylum in the name of Somalia, whilst referring to the Ethiopian man whose real name is believed to be Hamdi Isaac, arrested in Italy disguised as a Somali refugee with the name Hussain Osman. Furthermore, the connection that was made with Al Qaida was disproved too, as we were told that the alleged terrorists were probably home grown and disenfranchised youth. Some of them had criminal records and were in British prisons at some point and from British foster parents.

One British expert on African affairs commented: "It must have been unique for an Ethiopian, Eritrean and Somali to be together in this". What is even strange is that the fifth man is said to be Manfo Kwaku from Ghana, a country that has not been previously indicated as part of the terrorist world. In effect one does not need to have inquisitive or analytical minds to be sceptical about the collectivisation and the disproportional aspects of terror crimes.

The questions that linger in the minds of many citizens around the globe include: What is the connection between Islam and terrorism? Are Muslim countries and Muslim people around the world regarded as potential terrorists? Since when have madressas become breeding grounds for future terrorists and why? Bear in mind the fact that most of the present day Muslim countries were under European rule, notably the British, and that the madressas existed before, during and after the post independence years (the last 1400 years). As much as the madressas are criticised, Evangelical Christian groups have been given more then £1.3m by the Government to work with young people. The Department for Education runs courses for children and teenagers and youth support groups have given to proselytising Christian organisations, including the Crusaders. The grants from the government's National Voluntary Youth Organisation funding scheme far outstrip cash to Muslims or secular ethnic minority groups. The energetic evangelical organisation the Message Trust, which proclaimed it "has a vision to give every young person in the Greater Manchester region repeated and relevant opportunities to accept Jesus", gained £168,201 for a joint venture with project Caleb, which works with young people released from prison. Black leaders questioned yesterday why evangelical groups have received so much cash whilst youth groups working with disaffected young people in rundown black areas have not been supported" [75]

Is it justifiable that all Christians or Jews for that matter be held accountable for the crimes committed by a few of them? Is it wise for the British prime minister to summon Muslim leaders and to involve them in crimes they didn't commit? One Somali religious expert who gave an interview to the BBC Somali service in Bush House London mentioned that, "since it is not logical to blame all Christian Catholics as paedophiles, it is equally incorrect to link Islam with terrorism".

In the United Kingdom, an 18 year-old daughter is independent from her own family. How on earth would one expect people of different continents, cultures and class distinctions as well as economic and social disparities to be blamed for acts committed by criminals? With respect, one may not necessarily dispute the existence of criminals and crimes, even though many Muslims and non-Muslims doubt the validity of Al Qaida terror operations and the magnificence of their networks. Nonetheless, the irony is the clumsiness of the whole affair both from the police side and the alleged terrorists' side, not to mention the religious brand of the terror crimes. The questions arising include: If the terrorists were religiously and politically motivated, why did the bomb attacks take place in the parts of London predominantly occupied by Muslims and not in the more affluent and decision making areas of the capital and how could the criminals have been so clumsy as to leave their identities and belongings behind? On the other hand, the British police were not renowned for trigger-happy shoot-to-kill attitudes, so why the Brazilian Jean Charles de Menezes was mistakenly killed and what was the need to shoot him so many times? If he was considered a terrorist, why was he only dangerous to passengers in the underground but not to the bus passengers in that the police allowed him to board a bus before reaching the underground station? These observations are not new and were raised by analysts and amateurs alike. Such questions do not only engage brainstorming, but have been inadequately answered. The motives behind the established anti-Islamic terminology also need to be identified, not necessarily to appease Muslims, but to safeguard multiculturalism and mutual respect. It is indeed in the interest of harmonious progressive societies and inevitably beneficiary to all.

According to an article by Richard Ford and Stewart Tendler in The Times newspaper London on August 3, 2005, religious hate crimes soared by almost 600 percent in London alone since people attacked mosques and insulted Muslims. According to the Scotland Yard figures released on the 2nd of August 2005, 269 offences motivated by faith based hatred were reported since the 7th of July bomb attacks in London.

George Monbiot, who is a British writer and an environmentalist, in his article in the Guardian newspaper on August 9, 2005, page 17, entitled "The new Chauvinism," made the following comments: "Out of the bombings a national consensus has emerged: What we need in Britain is a renewed sense of patriotism. The right-wing papers have been making their usual noise about old maids and warm beer, but in the past 10 days have been joined by Jonathan Freedland in the Guardian, Tristram Hunt in the New Statesman, the New Statesman itself and just about everyone who has opened his mouth on the subject of terrorism and national identity. Emboldened by this consensus, the Sun now insisted that anyone who isn't loyal to this country should leave it. The way things are going, it can't be long before I'm deported...."

In a stark contrast, on 3rd August 2005, the conservative party shadow home secretary, David Davis, was reported to have told Muslims that they must do more to embrace common British values, including tolerance.

One Somali woman who used to be a lecturer in the then Mogadishu National University stated the following: "I find it difficult to understand why 'blaming the immigrants'. The British were in my country for more then 70 years without a visa and permission from our side; they did not engage our way of live. The social anthropologists were trained to support the colonial office. I think people should see the wider picture and relations between causes and effect."

Also, an elderly Somali woman said the following: "In my part of Somalia during the civil war Siyad Barre's administration hired (or was it aid) white South African mercenaries. Three of them were carrying British passports. Those British men bombarded my city and killed many civilians. They even followed us when we left the city; their involvement in the war maximised the deaths, civilian casualties and destruction of properties. That does not make us lump good British people with criminal British people. I may add that we Somalis are renowned for being proud and hospitable people. Because we suffered different wars, that does not mean we should be an easy target and a scapegoat. No situation is permanent and we must record who did what against us in times of civil strife. I say, as much as it is expected to be a good guest one should be also a good host. Otherwise one should not be welcomed in the first place. So in some ways we think the west is more developed and in another ways I think we are more advanced".

A Somali single mother in London had this to say: "There is a lot of talk that we Somalis have been welcomed and supported by the system but nobody talks about the hidden human cost. I am a mother of five, two sons and three daughters. My husband was a professional surveyor and I was a diplomat commercial attaché to a Somali Embassy. When I arrived in London my children encountered a lot of racism, one of my sons is named Mohammad and that some times makes it worse. All teachers are obviously not racist but one particular male teacher used to send my son out of the class … eventually that kind of attitude affects children's future. My son is now in prison. When I was in Somalia, I only heard political prisoners, thieves and mad people were supposed to be behind bars. Now underage people are locked up. There are many other unpleasant influences like that of tough surroundings and so on… I rather we all are shipped back…"

Many Somalis argue that before the civil war the reputation of the Somalis was that of being proud warriors but since the destruction of the country and the refugee influx some journalists from the host countries seem to be selective in concentrating on negative publicity against the Somalis. Hardly anybody gives coverage to the root cause of the Somali plight and not many incorrect reports have been taken to court on a fault accounts.

One Somali man in London commented about assimilation and terrorism issues, and said the following: "Visits were made to Somalia and local authorities were cooperating with the groups who visited the country. They included some CNN journalists. On their return they were convinced that Somalia does not host foreign fighters. In Mogadishu, we Somalis are reluctant to visit on security reasons, let alone being a safe-haven for foreigners.

It is rather contemptuous how some of the media attacks us...With regard to blaming us for less integration in the UK, it is not difficult to explain: For instance, if I come to your own house and you lock some rooms in the premises, then one day you wake up, suddenly demand why I shouldn't occupy those rooms; that is obviously illogical. I'm talking about the class system here (London). In places where immigrants can more easily work as professionals like the US and the Gulf States one would find Somali doctors, economists and other professionals practising their own professions and that includes other immigrants whether they are Muslims or non-Muslims. So who is to blame for social exclusions of immigrants? I believe that in Great Britain many professionals from the immigrant communities settled with less for employment opportunities and if you have a Muslim name it is twice as difficult."

Generally speaking, people to a certain extent retain their culture. Hence the British also did not adopt local people's cultures and traditions enthusiastically. The British Prime Minister Mr. Blair is expected to be enlightened enough in appreciating diversities in today's world.

At any rate, labelling political activists as terrorists is not a new phenomenon; neither are draconian laws and exiling active individuals. In colonial times, the British authorities in Somalia exiled some Somali leaders to other places including the Islands of Seychelles and Yemen. The British also introduced and implemented draconian laws in the Somali regions of the northern frontier district of Kenya. The successive Kenyan governments then endorsed those laws while those draconian laws were practiced at peripheral areas in the colonies. At best, however, mainland UK has been considered very much a place of law where people could appeal to courts against executive judges. The belief is that the UK is strong enough to be seen to be tolerant.

A Somali woman who was born in Aden, Yemen named Zeinab Dhadhera says: "There were always rulers and ruled in this world even if it is in a small scale. If the American and the British seek to rule the world they must be equipped and responsible enough. When I hear the rhetoric of Bush and Blair

I often change the channel... I was in Aden during the struggle for independence, even though the British were colonialist, but still they earned our respect for some reason. For instance if someone entered the mosque for amnesty, the British officers used to wait outside and respect the local beliefs. I remember a young activist who entered my father's house and the authorities waited until the morning and did not force their way in the house. There used to be some kind of gentlemanly attitude among the British, even if their polices were devastating for years to come, but now they are taking dogs to mosques and putting hoods to fathers heads in front of the children and the family. This kind of behaviour is inviting confrontations and resentments. It is as if it was pre-planned to provoke people..."

In this new scenario of robust hunting of the so called militants, who are said to be a threat to British culture and values, what effect would this have on the much admired British judiciary system of being "innocent until proven guilty"?

A British woman, Nuala Young, former lecturer at Brooks University Oxford, stated the following: "Tony Blair is the real threat to British cultural traditions because his government has encouraged racism and undermined the laws given to assure fairness to all in the country. Blair uses the old technique used by politicians in the last century of having a 'halting style' and speech to engage the sympathy of the listener. Because of this he comes across as a nice ...unthreatening ordinary man of the street. This style of speech covers the real presidential character of his role in the UK government..."

Other aspects related to race issues, identity, culture and loyalty-testing do not withstand the British tradition of enrichment from overseas and multiculturalism.

Somali wisdom says "Qof *weyn lama yidhahdo Afkaaga fur aan eelkahaga tiiriyee*: *Ceeb- baa- loo-ga-dhacayaa* " "Do not ask an elderly person to open the mouth to count his/her teeth. Such actions may lead you to shame."

In today's world of globalisation and interdependence, human connections and multiple identities seem to be more atmospheric than pinning down people's beliefs and loyalties.

4.2 Deceit!

In the case of Iraq and the issue of weapons of mass destruction, Hans Blix, the head of the United Nations (UN) weapons inspectorate stated that, "...there was no legal justification for war, the judgment of Bush and Blair was erroneous. It is as if they believed in witches and everything that came up was interpreted as supporting the existence of witches". [76] When I, interviewed Hans Blix in New York on September 2006, Mr. Blix mentioned to me that the findings of his team were basically ignored and that he produced a detailed account of his experiences in a book of which he gave me a copy. "Yes", said Mr. Blix, "Bush and Blair, if they saw a cat, they seemed to consider it as a smoking gun of some kind". A 1,200 word article signed by editors of one of America's most prestigious newspapers [New York Times] read "looking back we wish we had been more aggressive re-examining the claims as new evidence emerged or failed to emerge." [77]

However, even though the US and UK politicians adopted the phrase, "had I known then what I know now, I would not have voted for the war," neither of the two leaders (Bush & Blair) has expressed any regrets for waging war against Iraq. Instead the blame was laid on the failure of the international intelligence communities, and "... a new phrase entered the English vocabulary - 'Group thinking'" [78]. British Prime Minister Tony Blair was said to have acted in good faith. Needless to say, Saddam Hussein could have easily argued that he too must have had acted in good faith to acquire weapons for his national interests, bearing in mind that what enabled the US and UK to invade Iraq and attempt to shape the future of that country was not moral superiority but, obviously, weaponry superiority. Mr. Blair failed willingly and explicitly to apologise for taking part in a war that many conclude was an illegal war, including the Secretary-General of the United Nations, Kofi Annan. Instead, thousands of Iraqis seem to have been expendable, presumably for the removal of Saddam Hussein. However, it is apparent that more Iraqi lives were lost in the course of this war then under Saddam Hussein's rule. Furthermore, the prime minister's office admitted to the Observer newspaper in London, that "repeated claims by Tony Blair that 400,000 bodies had been found in Iraqi mass graves are untrue… "[79] Be that as it may, the Prime Minister argues his stance from the moral high-ground, proclaiming that he had taken a moral stand and extended democracy to Iraq. His foreign policy adviser, Robert Cooper, revealed differently by saying "Among ourselves we keep the law but when we are in the jungle we must also use the law of the jungle." Iraq may have been under the rule of a dictator for many years, but did she qualify for the description of jungle or was it falsely perceived as a jungle? An Iraqi priest in Baghdad at the Armenian Orthodox church said the following: "We have been living in Iraq for 100 years and have never had a problem between Muslims and Christians". When a church in Iraq was attacked in August, 2004, Samir Behnam, who was praying in the church, also said the following: "Whoever did this has no religion and principle… they want to create civil strife between us and the Muslims."[80] Moreover, at a conference at the Museum of London in June, 2004 on Iraq artefacts, an Iraqi woman stated: "I am Iraqi Arab Christian, my husband is Sunni, I am proud to be Iraqi, come what may, … my father-in-law who was Sunni was imprisoned by Saddam Hussein and was tortured by Kurdish collaborators…therefore a lot has been exaggerated. Everybody knows that Saddam Hussein was a secular and that one was only in danger if one opposed his regime and this, regardless of which sector of the community one came from". As for the Kurds during the Saddam regime in Iraqi, "chemical attack on the Kurds the US claimed that it had been carried out by the Iranians"[81] It is a fact that the USA was trading greatly with Saddam Hussein, one example among many being Dick Cheney, the Vice-President of the Bush administration, who served the petroleum corporation Halliburton as a chairman and during that time reportedly did a brisk $73 million in business with Saddam Hussein's regime.

An Iraqi shop owner in London expressed the following: "I was so much against Saddam, my views were let the devil come, anybody, but not Saddam. During the Iraq-Iran war, he treated many Shiites as if we were supporters of Iran but not Iraqis. He was brutal dictator, so it is all right to depose Saddam. It is even tolerable if they use the oil, but, excuse my language… to share my family and destroy my heritage that is altogether another matter". One US politician expressed in an interview during Iran-Iraq war in the 1980's that one major success for his party was the occurrence of the Iran-Iraq war. Does that reflect that the benchmark for the success of Bush's tenure is to be measured on the destruction of the Iraqi heritage, the conflict between the Shia and the Sunni and that US-occupied Iraq that harbours 12 percent of the world's known oil reserves accountable to the US lead forces? For how long would Bush administration-be able to mask the obvious and at what cost?

A Sunni Iraqi woman also said the following: "They first tried so hard to create civil strife between the Shiites and the Sunnis, then between the Muslims and Christians. They failed both times. At present they are working on how to create more problems between the administration they erected and rest of the Iraqi community …we know whose hands are there but the truth will prevail; sooner than expected perhaps".

One of the Shiite fighters in Najaf was reported by Ghaith Abdul for the Guardian newspaper to have said: "I will fight them even with my bare hands."[82]

A West Indian man who runs a coffee shop in London saw the cover page of one of the newspapers and stated the following: "Look at this picture of the burning holy cities and photo of Muqtada al Sadr. They deposed Saddam and found no weapons of mass destruction. Why are they killing Iraqis still and destroying their religious places? Iraq has thousands of years of history and wealth of its own. To me these people are racist they are not even after the oil! They do not want to see other people enjoying their culture. To me anybody who is a racist has an inferiority complex."

Nuha al- Radi, an Iraqi artist, wrote before she died, aged 63, "I must say that, as occupiers, the US are a most inefficient lot...Since we are to learn the American way of life, and suing is a hundred percent of it, we should start suing the US and the coalition for making war under false pretence. I don't think the Americans have a clue about this country or what to do with it."[83]

Even though it is believed that the sectarian killings in Iraq bore the hallmarks of civil war, undoubtedly Iraqis continue to display a national struggle that greatly emasculates Bush's ambition on the region by and large. It was argued that the removal of Saddam Hussein and dismemberment of the Sunni authorities could pacify Iraq. On the contrary, the Shia cleric Muqtada al-Sadr demonstrates one of the strongest oppositions against the American occupation. For the first time in 2007, a survey in Iraq showed that the majority of the Shia approve of armed struggle attacks on the Coalition Forces. Paradoxically, despite the fact that the War in Iraq is increasingly unpopular in the US and prominent persons raised their concerns against the war, the US Iraq study group recommended setting a timetable for withdrawal and the American electorate expressed their discontent with the war by voting for Democrats that dominate the Senate, but Bush continues to downplay the catastrophe. The US president announced sending more than 20,000 US troops to Iraq. After four years on the course, Bush seems to be recapturing Iraq by telling the world "...This would result in our troops being forced to stay in Iraq even longer and confront an enemy that is even more lethal" and the need for more US troops, Bush argues, is helping the Iraqis to stop the sectarian killings. Nonetheless, Frederick Kagan at the American Enterprise Institute, the institute is expected to have an influence on the Bush administration, stated: "We have to keep in mind that we face an enemy here that adapts to our strategy. If we do a short surge they will just wait us out and we need at least 18 months". The US ambassador to the United Nations, Mr. Bolton also stated an interview with Aljazeera Television "... it is not our interest on the Shia Sunni conflict once Saddam Hussein has been eliminated...."

Saddam Hussein has ruled Iraq with an iron fist. His record of human rights abuse against the Iraqi people, his invasion and the aggression against Kuwait plus his miscalculation of taking his people to war with Iran are also well known. Many Iraqis,too, argue that it was unwise of him [Saddam Hussein] to have fallen into the traps of engaging the then wars against Iran and invading Kuwait despite genuine grievances and conflicts of interests in both cases. But generally Iraq was a secular state in many ways, as has been known, there has not been any connection between Saddam Hussein and America's wanted list of Al Qaida. However, Iraq with its heritage was one of the places in the world where intellectuality, elaborate rituals, epic tales and poems, spirituality and classical traditions continued to remain unbroken. The elegance and luxurious places of Saddam Hussein's palaces were reflections of the grandeur-evolved culture of historical backdrop from Mesopotamia to Babylon to Baghdad. Victimising a whole nation for one man is nothing more than a war tactic.

The present day Bush/Blair war methodology on Iraq echoes that of Byzantium when Italy was invaded. There are historical comparisons of the sort as the following quotation indicates when Alaric of the Gothic Byzantium was to invade Italy: "The new century ...began with a bang. In the early summer of 401 ...he had left friends and enemies alike...spreading terror from the walls of Constantinople to the southern Peloponnese; ...he had also shown something else; that he was not fundamentally hostile to the Roman Empire. The truth, indeed, was quite the contrary. Alaric fought ...to establish a permanent home for his people within it, ...he would be granted high imperial rank... however, he changed his tactics. His purpose, he told the Romans, was not to put their city to fire and the sword but simply to overthrow Honorius, (who was their leader) now the single obstacle to peace in Italy. If they agreed, they must declare their emperor deposed and elect a more reasonable successor. He, for his part, would lift the siege forthwith. But Honorius, effectively defenceless, insisted on defiance"[84]

The similarities between Bush's wars on Iraq and the medieval wars are acute. For instance, when Bush stated that, "we must be ready to attack in any dark corner of the world," and he is fighting against those evils, this is very similar to what Constantine the Great stated a long time ago, as follows: "With such impiety pervading the human race, and the state threatened with destruction, what relief God devised?...I myself was the instrument he chose ...Thus, beginning at the remote Ocean of Britain, where the sun sinks beneath the horizon in obedience to the law of nature, with God's help I banished and eliminated every form of evil then prevailing, in the hope that the human race, enlightened through me,..."[85] (Constantine the Great quoted by Eusebius, De Vita Constantini, and 11, 28).

Moreover, in 1898 U.S President William McKinley said the following about his involvement in the Philippines at the time: "God had given the order for the U S to remain in the Philippines to civilise and Christianise its inhabitants." McKinley said he spoke with God on a midnight stroll down the halls of White House. Over a century later, the same argument prevails. "President Bush swears God is on his side in the conquest of Iraq."[86]

Furthermore, it was not the first time that a leader of a nation or a group was identified as a wanted man, dead or alive, because of acquiring weapons to strike. For instance, in the 1890's and during the colonial period in Tanzania, East Africa, a warrant was passed to capture dead or alive chief Mkwawa Munigumba of the Uhehe tribe. The chief was fighting against the European occupation, but was found dead. He committed suicide before he was caught. They cut his head off and took it to Europe to analyse the brain. They thought that he was not African because he could make guns, the way he organised his platoon and the tactics he used.

As for the analogy with the Crusades referred to when President Bush stated that, "This is a Crusade war", when the fourth Crusade in the Holy Land waged war against other Christians, "the predominant motive for the attack by Christians against Christian was greed. When they attacked Constantinople, they broke into the city and took possession of it.... The Emperor Alexius V fled and was later killed in Greece. There followed one of the most systematic lootings in history. Countless treasurers were stolen ...nothing was spared - not precious relics of Christ, nor the mosaic of the Church of Holy Wisdom, nor the tombs of the Emperor [But]...unlike the western Crusades of 1204, the Turks left much of the city alone. Indeed, the Sultan had a soldier flogged for trying to break up a mosaic in the Church of Holy Wisdom."[87]

To rekindle the Crusades and to glorify their past signifies moral degradation and intellectual retardation among other horrific historical legacies of the Crusades, including the practice of barbecuing children and occasionally eating their flesh. Those acts shocked Muslims of the time whose leader, Saleh Al Din Ibn Ayyub, was much admired by even his enemies. He was regarded as not only intelligent and tolerant, but a respectful man, polite with a moral superiority and discipline guided by gentle but powerful pursuit of the law. In the 1187 war between the Muslims and the Crusaders, Saleh Al Din, the Muslim leader, shocked the Christian Europeans by not taking revenge after his Muslim army defeated the Crusaders and took over the holy city of Jerusalem. He not only spared the Christian heritage in Jerusalem, but he told Christians that those who wanted to could stay and continue practising their religion with dignity. The second Crusade was also defeated. Many of the later Crusaders had converted to Islam and never returned. Those who returned adopted a culture that they found richer and superior to that of Europe. They brought with them knowledge of high Islamic culture and a taste for Muslim cuisine.

Furthermore, the neo-conservative hawks in America are said to have sought to establish what they called "Pax Americana" around the world. The Project for New American Century (PNAC) thinkers have developed what they call the "democratic domino theory in which, after the occupation of Iraq, the nations of Iran, Syria, Saudi Arabia, Lebanon, the PLO, and finally Sudan, Libya, Yemen, and Somalia will capitulate ...North Korea and some say China."[88]

On March 19, 2003, Michael Leaden of the influential right-wing think tank - the American Enterprise Institute (AEI that also houses PNAC) said "Iraq is a battle, not a war..."[89] and to win the war apparently includes occupying those nations.

"Richard Perle of the Pentagon advisory group the Defence Policy Board and AEI member says that, "to those states, we could deliver a short message, a two word message: 'you are next'"[90] Another PNAC signatory, Norman Podhoretz who also quantified the list of countries that the United States reports as axis of evil, says in his journal commentary on September 2002 at bottom, "This action is about the long over-due internal reform and modernization of Islam. The drive behind this war is ideological in nature, a crusade to "reform" the religion of Islam as exists in both government and society within the Middle East. Once this is accomplished, the road to empire will be open..."[91]

Therefore, it is not surprising when the Navy Chaplain, Lieutenant Wayne Hall of Oklahoma City told the US Marines during one of their assaults on Fallujah, in Iraq while blessing them, "Today is Palm Sunday, the day of Jesus triumphal entry into Jerusalem, where he broke the bounds of hell. Tonight commences your triumphal entry into Falujah, a place in the bounds of Hell. This is a spiritual battle and you Marines are the tools of mercy." As Lt Hall invoked the Holy Spirit, the Marines all dropped to one knee and bowed their heads, removing their bush or field caps as they did so."

Prime Minister Blair used the term "evil ideology". President Bush also said it openly on the television, addressing "Islamo-fascists". This kind of language is not expected to come from heads of government who attempt to rule the world, but it is more of the BNP (British National Party) language. Whatever message they are sending, such an attitude does more damage to their credibility as leaders then does to Islam. It also signifies hate and conflict promotion. When the leader of the British Labour party complements the language of neo-conservatism in the USA, awareness must be raised for the future of liberal minds in the UK and the US.

Anti-Islamic sentiments based on fear more than facts are hardly new, but the language and the wordings are different. Sir Henry

Campbell Bannerman, the then Prime Minister of Britain [1905-08], stated the following: "There are people who control spacious territories teeming with manifest and hidden resources, the intersections of world routes. Their lands were the cradles of human civilisations and religion, have one faith, one language, one history and the same aspirations. No natural barriers can isobaric people from one another...if, per chance, this nation were to be unified into one state; it would put the fate of the world into its hands and would separate Europe from the rest of the world. Taking considerations seriously, a foreign body [perhaps Israel] should be planted in the heart of this nation to prevent convergence of its wings in such a way that could exhaust its powers in never–ending wars. I serve as springboard for the west to gain its coveted objects". (See more on htp/www.islam channel. TV/forums...05/08/2005).

Unlike Bush and Blair, Sir Henry Campbell Bannerman did not deny the civilisation and the embodied knowledge of Islam, but expressed his fear for the enormity and the combined wealth of civilisation and geographical location renown of the Muslim world.

The stumbling point is therefore how far the Bush/Blair pre-emptive war of conquest for self-defence differs from the aims and appetite of the colonialist wars. It is worth reflecting on early attempts with regard to safeguarding the national interest and the sovereignty at risk. In 1963, the US's top military brass presented J. F. Kennedy with plans for operation North Woods, calling for a phoney terrorist campaign, complete with bombing, hijackings, plane crashes and dead Americans to provide "justification for an invasion of Cuba". One example (in a long list) goes as follows: " We could blow up a US ship in Guantanmo Bay and blame Cuba... Use of MIG type aircraft by US pilots could provide additional provocation. Harassment of civil air attacks on surface shipping and destruction of US military drone aircraft by MIG type planes would be useful as complementary actions. An F-86 properly painted would convince air passengers that they saw a Cuban MIG, especially if the pilot of the transport were to announce such fact...however, reasonable copies of the MIG could be produced from US resources in about three months

...US military intervention will result from a period of heightened US-Cuba tensions which place the United States in the position of suffering justifiable grievances. World opinion and the United Nations forum should be favourable, affected by developing international image of the Cuban government as rash and irresponsible, and as alarming and unpredictable threat to the peace of the western hemisphere"[92] (See more on unclassified documents JCS /1969? 321, 12 march 1962 page2165 Cuba project)

As for the issue of democracy and self-determination in Iraq, the following quotation explains that there have been similar cases of the sort during the British colonial presence in Iraq and collapse of the Ottoman Empire in 1918. When the British authorities were to reshape Iraq those attending that meeting included the then British Foreign Secretary Lord Balfour, who expressed the view that "it would be unwise to become pedantic about self-determination because it was inapplicable to wholly barbarous, undeveloped and un-organised Black tribes", to which Lord Cecil added that, "whilst self-determination should be an indication ... we should not attempt to leave it to the population to say." T. E. Lawrence said, "Self determination has been a good deal talked about. I think it is a foolish idea in many ways."[93]

In the current occupation of Iraq, Lt-Col. Nathan Sassaman, US Battalion Commander was quoted to have said: "With a heavy dose of fear, violence and a lot of money for projects, I think we can convince these people that we are here to help them"[94] [New York Times, 7/12/04].

The dilemma against the Iraqi army by the occupying force is also not new as the following quotation explains: In 1941The British (Foreign office asked Cornwallis to present his views and recommendations on the issues, particularly about steps which could be taken to covert the(Iraqi) army into forces capable of performing some functions useful to our(British) cause in the future ...Cornwallis asserted that he had spoken separately about the matter with Regent, the prime minister and the Minister of foreign affairs. The latter stressed: All unsuitable officers were being weeded out and replaced by trustworthy men. According to Cornwallis, much of the army is sullen and in no mood to obey unpleasant orders and the Government are dealing with them very gingerly…Perhaps however the purge should be carried still further and the army substantially reduced in size by the disbandment of the most unreliable elements" See more on Foreign office 371/27074-E2795, 3 June1941 and PhD thesis by Ibrahim Al-Aqidi.

There are more examples of deceit, contradictions and duplicities in the international world of power politics in which the truth has been masked for political ends and ulterior motives. For example, during the Suez crisis in December, 1955, the then British Prime Minister Eden told Parliament that Britain would 'assist Israel if she were attacked or assist an Arab country if she were attacked by Israel'. "Never before had he claimed that Egypt was not covered by this guarantee, yet now he was trying to twist things so that, instead of going to the aid of the victim of an aggressor, we would claim the right to assist the aggressor by attacking his victim. Instead of acting under the terms of the Tripartite Declaration 'to resist any attempt to change the existing armistice frontiers between Israel and the Arab States by force of arms' we were actively encouraging such a change by offering to lend the force of our own arms to that of Israel."[95] He added, "For during the night of October 31-November 1, British aircraft, in fulfilment of our pledge to Ben Gurion (the then Israeli prime minister) bombed four of Egyptian airfields – Almaza, Inchass, Abu Sueri and Kabrit and early the next morning followed up these raids with attacks on a total of nine Egyptian aerodromes." The Royal Air force had kept Eden's promise to the Israelis, who could now continue their advance across Sinai, safe in the knowledge that Nasser could neither retaliate against their cities nor harass their progress in the field".[96]

Furthermore, in 1954 Egypt cracked an Israeli military cell of Egyptian Jews who firebombed sites frequented by westerners to embarrass Cairo and stop it nationalising the Suez Canal. Two were hanged, one committed suicide, six others were jailed and (Israel) Defence Minister Pinhas Lavon quits though denies authorising the plot [in more recent times 2004]. The Prime

Minister of New Zealand angrily denounced Israel and imposed diplomatic sanctions on it after two suspected Mossad agents were jailed for six months for trying on false grounds to obtain New Zealand passports. "This type of behaviour is unacceptable internationally by any country. It is a sorry indictment of Israel that it has again taken such actions against a country with which it has friendly relations," said prime mister Helen Clark.[97]

At a Labour Party conference in September 2004, the prime minister's speech for the party included trusting him and that, in order to safe-guard democracy in the UK, his government should address the security and peace in Iraq. Moreover, an Iraqi woman was given the platform of the Labour party conference in order to extend her support to the prime minister, saying that he (Mr. Blair) strongly freed her from the dictator in Iraq. This is in striking contrast to the view expressed by Half Zangan from Iraq, who is a writer an activist and was imprisoned by Saddam Hussein. She wrote the following: "I hate everything Saddam has done but I also detest Bush and Blair …Beware of a man with a vision so does (sic) Tony Blair. He also asks history to be his judge. He has also taken away our voice, the voice of dissent. We sent a letter signed by 160 artists, academics and intellectuals. He ignored it, but quoted from a group claiming to speak for all Iraqis. It is strange to feel the same things happening in democracy that happened in Iraq…it is as though I never came out of prison, even though I have been here (England) 25 years…"[98]

As for the gravity of events since September 11-2001; to start with, the US authorities told us (citizens of the globe) that there are Muslim terrorists who definitely carried out those horrific attacks of the Twin Towers. Then we were introduced to what are famously known as the "Al Qaida terror networks" that lead waging war against Afghanistan. The other threat that gained popularity was the ill-judged Iraqi possession of weapons of mass destruction (WMD). It led to regime change and democratisation, followed by events in London and the misidentification of those who allegedly carried out the London bomb attacks was presumably allowed to circulate. The insult to immigrants was upbeat and the quality of journalism slipped down in many ways. All and all, the current scenario of post-modern power politics that some see as chess and drama seems to have leapt into "evil ideology" amalgamated by directing the fight against "fundamentalists and extremists", loyalty-testing, integration, deportation and the introduction of new legislation that may lead to draconian laws as practised by the UK authorities in East Africa in the last century.

It is of paramount importance, therefore, to conclude that this kind of contradiction would have a big impact on trust. For instance, who created "Al Qaida", who financed them, who trained them and how did the notions of Osama bin Laden and global terrorism come to light? Whilst historical evidence suggests that it has been the USA that spearheaded the formation and the operations of Al Qaida for its advantage against the then power of the USSR, the motivation behind anti-Islamic structured language raises further questions. For instance, the word fundamentalism has been misused. Fundamentalist is to know the essence and the true pillars of what one is practising, e.g. one cannot be a good doctor with out knowing the fundamentals of medicine, as suggested by one expert. Therefore no Islamic or Christian fundamentalist could possible kill innocent people. One is told that a good Christian indeed should turn the other cheek, let alone wage pre-emptive wars. However, if there is such a thing as original "Sin" and a retaliated second "Sin", the proposition could be that state-structured terrorism evokes the "individual and group" structured counter terrorism. In addition, the use of the term Islamic extremists, too, seems invalid in substance and decorative in meaning. Partly because the nature of "occupation" in one's land causes the formation of "resistance", it is commonly known that one man's terrorist is another man's freedom fighter. There have been a number of former heads of state, including Nelson Mandela of South Africa, who was regarded as terrorists in their struggling years. Partly because of this, the prevailing ambiance of geographical areas blanketing terrorism sharpens the phenomenon of a political socio-economic discontent rather then dismissing it in an abstract form of "Islamic extremism".

Another area of concern is the reticence of Mr. Blair when he says: "our morals and values... way of life" and so on. The contradictions in these aspects are that the existence of universal definitions of what good morals and values are does not have geographical distinctions. It is accepted wisdom that good or bad people do not have boundaries. In other words, they are to be found everywhere. The validation of a common, homogeneous, static local or indigenous way of life is also debatable, especially when the United Kingdom has a history of looking overseas for labour and economic ventures. Indeed, in every country around the globe there exist the privileged elite, the not so privileged and, in some cases, impoverished masses.

In any given society, there are social economic stratifications and sects within a religion, including Christianity; not to mention that Christianity itself has been imported from the Middle East. Also, values and practices are not symmetrical. Hence, within a nation, what someone champions another opposes. Thus, every culture encapsulates various cultures including the mainstream culture, which may be domineering but not necessarily depictive. In other words, the British class system itself derives from persons of different social and economical backgrounds. Social movements also influence cultures; so there are no monocultures within a group or a nation. How can one attempt to transform other cultures that are equally pluralist in nature unless the centre of concentration has empirical connections?

When President Bush made the statement that "you are either with us or against us" almost all the Muslim governments (who aren't necessarily Islamic states) ducked and no heroism has been entertained. Their actions were regarded as unpatriotic and predominately criticised by their own citizens. In retrospect, however, that action of stepping back at best allowed a space where the Bush administration's jingoism and contradictions on Iraq war and terrorism unfolded.

During the colonial period, the British line was very much one of association, whilst it has been the French who were to promote assimilation. In post-independence years, perhaps British foreign policy seems to have maintained good relations with selective dictators and sheikhdoms, whilst exercising open intellectual thinking, political liberalism parallel with conservatism and its record of imperialism. The conventional wisdom appears to be that the UK has been in a position of influence. Hence, allowing political dissidents to detoxify their brains and express ideas, not necessarily mainstreaming them, whilst not loosing the grip for the bigger picture of pursuing UK's economic interests according to Blair, rules have changed, we are told. The irony of controlling governments is one thing. Fighting against terrorism and maintaining security guidelines is necessary, but how can one control the feelings and the minds of fellow human beings whose ideas and attitudes are mostly shaped by the ever growing unprecedented media of all kinds? One is referring to the hate laws. The human feelings of "hate" and "love" can't be regulated by legislation, but only by deeds. Actions speak louder than words.

One Nigerian political scientist made the following comments: "When the British media talks about Africa they often concentrate on the negative side; things like starvation, witchcraft and circumcision. When they talk about China it is often about human rights and how China is backward along those lines, as for India and sub-continent it is often about child labour, floods black market. With regard to Muslims, it is about terrorism and Al Qaida and personally I don't believe that Al Qaida exists as it is often presented. However the truth of the matter is that, yes, times are changing and there are alternative media. People are not only in touch with their national media, but are also able to connect other nations' media. Therefore, when one engages negative publicists about other cultures and nations, at best there would be environments of antipathy"

In these times of media manipulation and under-rating Muslims, whether in subtle or in aggressive form, all this may rest upon short-term neutralisation. Hence, there are no mysteries to crack and Islam has been around for the last 1,400 years. In all those years there were the dynamics of legal and religious writing, secular literature, philosophers and thinkers. In the course of the Islamic empire there has not been a complex debate that has not been unravelled, whether in Baghdad, Cairo, Cordoba, Persia, Turkey, the Magrib or India.

As for the sequence of events, the historical setting of post-modernity has been the last century of colonialism and neo-colonialism that could be attributed to contemporary equity and ethical deficiency in today's world Since the Napoleonic times plus the later collapse of the Ottoman Empire, Arab and Muslim civilisation has been discontinued as an independent entity. The European colonial powers demarcated the present-day state borders in the region. Islamic supra-nationalism has been demolished. Therefore, the established modern state status quo has been maintained in the post-independence period. Most of the regimes in the region continued to be friendly with the US/UK and remained politically and economically non-resistant to the west. Secularism and different ideological thought have been entertained in different times in the Middle East and nearby regions. In retrospect, some Muslim states as well as individual elites proclaimed socialism and communism to be adapted. At best, however, Islamic studies and religious adherence continued to function in the form of educational and human development standards. It is a known fact that none of the Muslim states were in effect engaging Islamic Law in its totality. Nor do they embrace Islamic civilisation as such. To a certain extent people turned their backs on their traditional wisdom and Islamic jurisprudence. In many ways they have been under tremendous influence from the west for so long and sought solutions in modernity and technological development, hence, the material power shifted into the west since the Renaissance and so on. As a result, the present-day Middle East is one created by the European powers of the time. So what significance would a "New Middle East" reveal? Is it faith-based confrontation, as mentioned above? Is it capitalistic venture to control the potential wealth of the Muslim habitat in those countries, or is it a semi-sick excitement of one having weaponry capabilities to annihilate?

The power of the west did not derive only from military conquest and the World Bank IMF structural adjustments. Many attuned with its claim to the ideologies of pluralism, pragmatism, diversity and giving a space to humanism and freedom of expression, supported by the media and western film industry that facilitated the traffic of the South to the North in which many people from the developing world risk their lives to reach the North

As one Somali man who was a refugee and then returned voluntarily put it: "You don't have to bring the slave trade with chains. These days one sells one's properties to reach the North. It was positive propaganda that brought us to search betterment. From the way things are progressing it will be hate propaganda that will make us return. Social anthropologists are not only from one side these days. We are observant too, and in due course follow the actualisation of what we have but fail to appreciate. Who knows? It may be a blessing in disguise."

Nonetheless, there is the school of thought that depreciates the idea that the west is to be blamed for the mischief of the south and it is worth noting the other viewpoints that mention the mistakes and weaknesses of the other side. Dr. S Ahmad, a Somali economist, expressed the following: "I have my reservations about blaming everything that goes wrong on the west, colonialism or imperialism, not to mention the US and the UK governments. Look at all these despots in the so-called developing world. For instance, how many African leaders give consideration on citizens' rights? They are often more concerned in power consolidation. As for the Arabs and the Muslims, it is common knowledge how thin the solidarities among them are.

"One is perfectly aware that there are Muslim states that give job priorities to non-Muslims and prefer to employ a secretary with no headscarf. I give you another example; when the Saudis were poor they used to predominantly rely on Somali livestock and fruits. Now the situation has changed. They rather go to Australia to commerce with livestock. If you ask a Saudi why they keep boycotting Somali livestock, they will tell you "the conspiracy theory": 'The 'Israelis are behind all this'. When the civil war broke out, the UK, Ethiopia and others welcomed Somali refugees. Personally I am very much thankful to the British for the special concessions that they give to the Somali refugees.

Even though we are members of the Islamic Conference and the Arab League, with the notable exception of Syria and the Sudan, who else allowed Somali children for free education and waiver visa for Somalis? How many occasions an Arab turned you down, wasted your time or terminated your contract without notice or worker's rights? How many Jewish lawyers took over the cases of the Somali refugees in Europe and in North America? Do you notice with most Gulf States they have more relations and employments with Delhi than with Islamabad? Are you aware the Arab rich who pay £2000 tip to restaurants in the west; do they remember the homeless children in Palestine? What about Iraq? The list could go on and on and I do not endorse for blind loyalties of all sides".

There is hardly an unturned stone on Arab weaknesses and how their disunity continues to backfire against their security and political development. Numbers of Arab thinkers do write if the Arab leaders would ever learn from their mistakes. However, one cannot suspend the root causes so to evolve.

Dr Ahmed's comments are proverbial but, with regard to the Somali issues unlike the then British authorities and the Ethiopian administration, the Arabs did not partition Somalia nor do they occupy Somali territories and they do not have ambition to frustrate a strong Somalia as evidence suggests. Lack of political coherence and failure in adapting effective mechanisms to abate aggression is one thing but obviously the Palestinian, Iraqi and Somali endeavours cannot be attributed to the Arabs and, for justice to prevail, it is irrelevant whether one supports or not. One argues, therefore, that generalisation is often unjust. The Arabs share the same language and perhaps could be a "Nation" but not one "Nation State". They reside in different countries. Each has its policies and priorities. They comprise people of different continents and also have different neighbours and historic influences. One can safely say they are classified as Arabic-phone, to consider them as one sovereign state is not right. Indeed it is a mistake often made to singularise Arabs as if they are one country or one group. Dr Kishore Saint of India at a conference in the Gandhi National Centre of Arts stated the following: "…But today dialogue between peoples is especially obstructed by racial an ethnic stereotypes that are created for political and military purposes, and that can be created overnight. Sociologists have shown that, in the United States before the Second World War, Arabs were perceived as good fighters and exotic desert-lovers with harem girls. Before World War II, there was little American political involvement in the Middle East. The defence of Israel and the struggle for control of the oil reserves changed all that…as for the media, a population that had no idea at all who or where the Hutus or Kosovo's or Tamils are a week later have a fixed image of them as people with whom dialogue is impossible". Whilst propaganda and misinformation seem to be part of modern warfare, providing a less balanced picture of issues could contribute to less understanding between groups and nations.

With regard to the African despotic regime, British barrister Peter Roth, QC asked me what I think about not intervening in oppressive regimes such as Rwanda, The Sudan and Mugabe of Zimbabwe, then added "condemning intervention is one thing but is there a third option." "Don't get me wrong," Peter says, "I am not talking about Iraq. For that, to express disapproval seems to be easy." Does one have a solution?" It is rather tricky. It is certainly a question that needs to be explored by a wider audience. However, there are different forms of intervention and different ways of intervening. There is also a difference between intervention and assistance. The word intervention could mean intrusion or impediment, but it could also mean mediation and arbitration.

"There is positive intervention and negative intervention. Dictators vary too, locally carved or internationally imposed. Local traditions are generally equipped to unseat unpopular regimes. They are also in position to amend their differences and there have been successful cases. The controversial ones are the favoured dictators or those discriminated against in time and place by the third parties. It is therefore a moral responsibility to engage, diagnose and provide proper treatment. Right intervention certainly has its merits. On the other hand, one cannot ignore the obstacles in making headway and the constant interruption of local and regional balance of power to determine the outcome. What about the mercenaries and coup plotters whose moral benchmark is to make money come what may? Who gives those dictators weapons, bribes them and helps them to stay on power? Africa is not capable of making weapons and they are never short of military hardware. It is also the case that most African dictators are criticised when they are not favoured any more or fall from power. Africa also is subjected to companies from the developed world who executes toxic waste dumping. That is not to say that there are no local collaborators, but the concern is the twist of the community fabric by equipping the wrong ones against the right ones.

In the programme "Who Gives Aid to Whom", the late president Nyerere of Tanzania, East Africa mentioned how Africa providing cash crops to the developed world contributes to the food shortage in Africa, and when countries like the US bring wheat surpluses in harvesting times, how that affects the morale of the local farmers. President Nyerere also mentioned in that programme that countries like Tanzania do not have a say in fixing the price of their own cotton. Once the cotton reaches places like the City of London, a Tanzanian may not even afford the cost of cotton shirts and added that there may be no more milk in the African Cow and that the likes of the IM F and the World Bank are now milking the blood of that "Cow".

A Ghanaian woman who works for the UN expressed how credit is not given to African products as well as African intelligentsia and gave the following examples: "The Swiss chocolate is the West African Coco. The South African diamonds are referred to as Belgian diamonds. How many times does a high-level consultant give credit to his or her local partners?" She added "Does anybody listen to the millions of people in the West who are a focal majority and advocate for fair trade, peace and a just world"

To sum up, therefore, how progressive are the powers that revisit ancient, medieval and colonial wars to settle twenty-first century confrontations? How democratic is the democracy that allows the British National Party (BNP) to operate on the grounds of freedom of speech and then silences their counterparts in the Arab and the Muslim World? One could argue that the majority of them had their views formulated and shaped by the constant propaganda attacks against Muslims; for instance, when Lieutenant-General William Jerry Boykin told a church congregation in Oregon that the US was at war with Satan who wants to destroy his country's Christian army. This man did not face imprisonment, a death penalty or even house arrest, as was the case with Abu Hamza of the Finsbury Park Mosque in London. Moreover, The National Alliance, the largest Neo-Nazi Organisation in the United States, which said that they want to create a new government answerable to white people only, are seldom in the media limelight.

Paradoxically, when some of the western media air programmes that criticise both Arabs and other ethnic communities, those acts are to be seen as freedom of press but, when it is from the other side of the fence, it is propagated as hate incitement and threat to the 'national security'.

The theory does not match the practice. Whilst Bush and Blair are telling the world that they are exporting democracy 7000 miles to Iraqi, in practice the indications are that they are jeopardising democracy at home; democracy that was achieved through centuries of hard work in promoting civil liberties by men of courage and good will who challenged centuries of injustice and replaced laws in Europe with regard to executions and tyranny that prevailed in early times. It has been almost 350 years since imprisoning people without invoking the rule of law has been challenged. Indeed: "for the first time in the modern history of Britain are people imprisoned secretly and without trial."[99] The US Patriotic Act is also a severe blow to liberty, justice and human rights. Howard Zinn, a US professor-emeritus of political science at Boston University, wrote in an article in the Guardian newspaper on 12 August 2005: "It is not only Iraq that is occupied. America is too. The American International Report 2005 Guantanamo Bay has become the gulag of our times …when the most powerful country in the world thumbs its nose at the rule of law and human rights; it grants a license to others to commit abuse with impunity. The war on terrorism is not only a war on innocent people in other countries; it is a war on the people of the US on our liberties, on our standard of living. The country's wealth is being stolen from the people and handed over to the super rich. The lives of the young are being stolen"...[100] The Guardian newspaper in London also reported on 1st July 2004, that the US Pentagon make it clear that some parts of the American government want to use torture routinely as a deliberate instrument of policy.

In the final analysis, one could argue that there is no clash of civilisation, nor are there cultural paradigms that triggered world wide confrontation, but ostensibly there is greed, the desire to control and to have it all. Richard Happer of the Financial Times, expressing concern about China's growing trade and its economic expansion wrote: "The link between Brazil and China connects the biggest emerging market of the western and eastern hemisphere that could pose a challenge for the Bush administration with his obsession with the Middle East and the US myopic development in its own backyard." [101]

It is true that world trade is not a pyramid any more as Asia is rapidly industrialising and technology is disseminating fast. However, is breaking a nation a solution for sustaining power?

In a changing world, what will be the role of the United Nations? It is understood that the role of the General Assembly is diluted when it comes to conflict resolution between states or within states, whilst that of the Security Council is overwhelmingly reinforced and exercised. For this, the consideration of the Security Council's devices raises questions about the body's accountability, as it is not democratically represented. The political selectivity of the potential intervener in choosing its geographical area for intervention under the aegis of the Security Council is also apparent. Passing and demanding the fulfilment of resolutions in Iraq, Somalia or Syria, Iran, etc. and its reverse approach regarding Israel speaks for the criteria of neutrality and impartiality.

With regard to scoring contradictions, how can one engage policies of military intervention that involve loss of lives and destruction of infrastructures, yet not expect resent or, indeed, resist? How can one promote globalisation, strategic advances, acquisition of labour force and commodities and then complain about immigrants and multiculturalism, thus compromising tolerance and invoking protectionism? "Historically, all centres of grandeur cultures have been cosmopolitan in nature, with markets full of foreign merchants and whole quarters of settled foreigners. What we have come to know as distinctive and dominant civilisations in Egypt, Persia, China, Rome and Mongolia, were the result of drawing towards themselves resources, artefacts, inventions and concepts from the most diverse ethnic areas and cultures." [102]

With reference to the issues of the "free world" and the claims of civility and rule of law, not to mention morals and values, it is significant to explore whether the economic and technological advances of the west contributed to an ethical maturity. Or is it the old wisdom that power corrupts? Prime Minister Blair repeatedly talks about the "open society and free world". What does free world encompasses and how free is free? On the other side of the argument, who are the close societies? There is the school of thought that holds the view that the people in the developing world are more open, welcome strangers and are less reserved. Yes, the community bond is strong and you do not take your grandmother to an institution. Unpopular habits are deterred, not encouraged. Does that equal closer societies or is there more? Does free world include the ability to destroy the "Other"?

The current US and UK administrations seem to have undermined the most internationally and nationally known laws with regard to their activities in Iraq and the terrorism fiasco. Those include: the UN Charter and the issues of sovereignty, integrity and self-determination in the legality of war on Iraq. Under the Geneva Convention for the rights of the prisoners of war and the non-combating civilians, the responsibility of the occupying power, the obligations of the conqueror to the conquered and maintaining one's innocence until proven guilty in a court of law that are essential. In promoting international world government to dilute human rights and the rights to freedom of speech and so on, in countering terrorism, the US is engaging unofficial combat against Southern Somalia. What kind of morals justifies bloodshed?

It has been said that the Abu Ghraib prison abuse has been part of the Bush administration's war tactics and it was meant not only to subdue the prisoners and their families but a deliberate thing to send a message to demoralise and insult the Muslim ethos. In stark contrast, this action reveals the darker side of the perpetuators. The attitude of the likes of Rumsfeld and Dick Cheney tested the patience of the most sympathetic and it may well be the main factor that recruits young Arabs and Muslim resisters in Iraq today. It accentuates negative publicity and serves no pride to the community of the "coalition of the willing". It does not estrange the Muslims and the Arab communities only, but also the wider world community of decency.

Laureate George A. Akerlof, 2001 Economics Nobel prize-winner, said: "I think this is the worst government the US has ever had in its more then 200 years. It has engaged in extraordinary irresponsible policies, not only in foreign policies and economics but also in social and environmental policy. This is not a normal government policy. Now is the time for US people to engage in civil disobedience…"

The core argument in the context of contradictions is not only to exhibit the availability of ample contradictions in the form of action and oratorical embodiment, but also it is leading us in a grey area of bewilderment. Many African, Middle Eastern and Asian scholars have articulated the North South political and socio-economic disparities. So did liberals in the west and 60s trendiest who encouraged peace movements. All those achievements are challenged by the present climate of mobilising fear and hate.

Those who believe bullying nations is the only guarantee for future control of the globe are simply mistaken, partly because no one can upstage destiny and partly because, by unleashing total war, it could expedite the inevitable. The discourteous ambience and the speed in which events are developing plus the surrounding ambivalent tensions may lead to outright conflict. Indeed, primitivism may overtake progressivism and privileges may not be sustainable unless commonsense prevails. It may be never too late to amend mistakes.

There is no excuse for breaking nations to maintain supremacy. The human and the environmental costs are high. It is counter-productive and, at any rate, nobody can hold history.

All powers come and go. In time they all acquire their peaks and declines, with which they all make their mark and they leave that mark behind. The Bush/Blair war against Iraq will no doubt be remembered for the blunders in Baghdad, Falujah, Najaf and the sadomasochistic abuse in Abu Ghraib, as well as the abuse of prisoners in Guantanamo Bay and Afghanistan. The lack of respect for the human soul, the desire to humiliate and to show off, the profound absence of remorse or regret from Bush and Blair's international politicking; whose attitude is not justice-driven but image-driven, is a striking phenomenon. It is undoubtedly history in the making.

It is not only Saddam Hussein who was on trial; the US administration and the claimants of "civilisation" are on historical trial. People are watching and forming their opinions. The occupation forces' contradictions and evaded duties speak volumes about their morals and values. It breeds contempt and, subsequently, one could argue that Bush and Blair may have been successful in liberating the Arabs and the Muslim communities in the wider Muslim world, not from dictators and sheikdoms but from the perception of western civilisation, jurisprudence, concerns for human rights, fair trials and the like, that has been maintained for so long.

In short, what this era of arrogance and miscalculation facilitates could be to devalue western morals and values, in particular that of the US and the UK. It could encourage millions of Muslims and non-Muslims to revisit Islamic civilisation. That is long overdue. Subsequently it might well be an enlightening time for Islamic studies and Muslims by and large.

An English convert, T. Alan, stated the following: "I converted to Islam in 2003; I became aware of what I saw as propaganda in the press plus the news, and decided to read and study Islam. I was surprised and enlightened. I realised that Islam is a religion of peace and saw a purity that I had never seen in a religious book. I can safely say Mr. Bush and Mr. Blair showed me the path to Islam…"

As for the US; once a great power loses its powers of persuasion, influence and the capacity for civility, undermines deterrence and policies of détente, it categorically exhibits its hard power, the ability to annihilate and the willingness to destroy. Such a situation is a mark of a declining power. The liberal minded US citizens must challenge the Bush administration vigorously and urgently to regain their popularity and the US ideology of free world

The Italians say 'Semini vento raccogi tempesta' (If you sow wind, you get a storm).

It is true that in the then British Empire there were more Muslims then were Christians, but independence has been achieved, nobody can turn the clock back and in contemporary norms of international communalism nations prioritise with whom they see fit to engage relationships. In the long term, therefore, the tougher laws that Prime Minister Blair so eagerly advocates may not serve the future interests of UK. A lot of Muslim countries preferred the UK mainly because of familiarity and traditional links of some sort, but if tough measures mean legalising injustice, and then it will not be long before an exodus of people begins. Many students may decline to come and businesses may turn to face the east and China. Then what happens? Bombard every country that refuses to abide by selective resolutions?

An English writer on arts and culture in Oxford commented about Mr. Blair's policies in the UK and said the following: "Blair disappointed me and my generation, I am in my fifties, we anticipated that a young Blair will take Britain forward, instead he seems to be more conservative than the conservatives. I do not know, perhaps we think that we gave birth to the US and therefore pursue this "special relationship affair". It is madness. A lot of middle-class British people are leaving the UK. In due course this country will be left with the super rich and their servants..." Furthermore, academics and laymen alike share the belief that in twenty or so year's economical power may shift, slowly but surely, to Asia. Hence the present-day powers of the world should try to better their historical record. It is also important to embrace the natural ways in which global power shifts and rotates that are known to have been beyond human dictation. As times change, therefore, to age gracefully is very much recommended.

5. Chapter

In the aftermath of September 11, 2001, it has been the case that notorious barbarism and civilisation emerged as the key elements in the new war of terror. The Arab and Islamic aspects of the war on terrorism echoed as a clash of civilisation and cultural confrontation.

5.1 Who Civilised Whom?

The British Prime Minister Mr Blair states in some of his public speeches that, "Our way of life, morals, values and civilisations are under threat". Mr Blair says that he is not against Islam but he hardly indicates otherwise. In his speeches, when the prime minister talks about terrorism, he some how mentions Islam. That gives the impression that the two (Islam and terrorism) are interlocked.

Islam has been also relentlessly attacked in writing, in talk shows and in various speeches. It is a violent religion they say, archaic, medieval, and oppressive of women. Furthermore, President Bush stated prior the invasion of Iraq by the US led forces the following: "We must be ready to attack in any dark corner of the world." On another occasion Bush said, "This is a crusade war!"

In pursuit of the above issues let me shed light on who civilised whom. Who is terrorising whom and who fails to curtail the language of confrontation that makes plausible in a divisive world and the threat to world harmony?

To start with, let us define the word civilisation. The definition of the word civilisation refers to a particular period of time in particular part of the world. It also explains an advanced stage of social, moral and cultural refinement. In the process, civilisation evolves, emerges inter-woven and then yields conglomeration and hybridisation, whereby modernity replaces classicism. For that, there have been civilisation and knowledge borrowings between and amongst nations throughout history, as a result of which so many great empires rose and fell. Thus, one may argue that civilisations do not clash but complement, if not continue.

Therefore, let us throw light on whether Iraq could be a dark corner, or if the US is encountering one of the oldest civilisations in the world.

In Mesopotamia (present day Iraq), 5000 years ago Sumerians combined their skills to set up an organised state, where writing was invented "...Between the rivers Tigris and Euphrates lies a broad fertile valley that has a better claim than anywhere else on earth to be regarded as the birth place of civilisation. In the southern part of this long valley, an energetic and inventive people known as the Sumerians began to build the world's first cities 5000 years ago (3500-539 BC). They invented a system of writing, discovered bronze and they are the first people known to have used wheeled vehicles ...The Sumerians also waged the world's first wars, as distinct from tribal skirmishes."[103]

Furthermore, one of the remarkable city-states of the Sumerians was Mari on the middle Euphrates, "a city impressive for its size and regular plan. The remains of palaces, houses and workshops are laid out in orderly streets on a grid pattern like a modern city and there are fine sculptures, coloured frescoes and cemeteries. The women who are depicted in statues and frescoes wear long, flounced skirts, similar to those worn by the highborn women of Minoan Crete at about the same time. The main palace of Mari has 250 rooms, ranging from the residential quarters of the Royal Family to the school ...in these rooms were trained the boys who were to become civil servants, administering the territory of God and the King. Here also patient scribes and scholars copied poems, proverbs and palace accounts on tablets, of which some 20,000 have been preserved."[104] Historians described the Sumerians as gifted people who also knew algebra, human anatomy and surgery; and they were knowledgeable about medicines extracted from various plants, including myrtle and thyme. After the Sumerians, the Babylonians and the Assyrians succeeded them; whilst they inherited the literature of the Sumerians. They also added their contribution. "Copies of Sumerians and early Babylonian tablets kept and stored in libraries, ...and in time, much of this knowledge was passed on to the Greeks and the Romans, and so to western world."[105]

The Greeks included the Hanging Gardens of Babylon as one of the seven wonders of the world. It is also worthy to note that King Hammurabi, who ascended the throne of Babylon in 1792 BC on the middle Euphrates, "...was one of history's great lawgivers. A stone pillar, or stele, found at Susa and now in the Louvre in Paris, is inscribed with the details of his legal decisions, showing evidence of high standard of legal procedure which existed 15 centuries before the law of the Romans...the laws were just and reasonably humane. Women's rights were protected..."[106]

Furthermore, during the peak of the Islamic civilisation in 762, Caliph Mansur of the Abbasid dynasty transferred their capital from Damascus to Baghdad in Iraq, which was then considered a more central place. They then constructed a designed city that contained government offices, mosques, shops, baths, prisons, houses of officials and servants. In the middle of its perfect circle was the palace of the Golden Gate, surmounted by a great green dome. "...Each street assigned to dealers in one commodity. Market inspectors (*muhtasib*) kept an eye on quality, weights prices and stopped cruelty to animals. Baghdad and Basra thrived as centres of commerce. Most trade was in luxury goods, since every region was normally self-supporting in essentials ... From the Persian Gulf, ships sailed for China with camphor, ivory, copper, amber and rhinoceros horn, valued as an antidote to poisons and an aphrodisiac. To the markets of Iraq came gold and ivory from Africa, furs and textiles from Constantinople and Trebizond, on the Black Sea; carpets from Armenia, timber and iron from Europe, glass from Syria and also the cloth which is still called damask, after Damascus." It was then remarked that a "poor man in Baghdad is like a Qur'ān in the house of an atheist."[107]

However, Islamic civilisation was based on a multi-racial melting pot whose individual talent was encouraged by the pursuit of the Qur'ān and the *Ḥadīth* (reliably transmitted reports by the Prophet Muhammad of what he said, did or approved). Islam spread fast; faster than any other religion or power within a short period to three continents. During that period, Islamic powers were not using the language of conquest and catastrophes, but a language of universal brotherhood, peace, enlightenment and a culture that, unlike the Christian Europeans of the time, separates the divine from the human mind of reasoning. The most powerful weapons of Islamic civilisation were generosity, kindness, equality and unity, amalgamated with ingenious culture of literature and trade innovations. When Muslims entered a new place, the Arabic word "fatuh" was used, which means opening. One questions how far Prime Minister Blair is aware when he engages so often and so rigorously terms like open society versus close ones!

The author of "The Rising Tide of Islam Engulfed the Ancient World and Created a Universal Brotherhood" wrote the following about Islam (page 148,): "According to the tradition, Islam was spread by warriors holding the Qur'ān in one hand and sword in the other, but the picture is false …Islam had much to offer the faithful. It proclaimed that all men were equal before Allah, it promised paradise to true believers and it was tolerant enough to accept Moses and Jesus as prophets along with Muhammad. Once the Islamic Empire was established there was another incentive: To become a Muslim conferred full membership to flourishing community." Even when allegiance with the central government was not strong and there were feuds and break-away governors, "…Islam as religion and civilisation it gave rise, proved enduring. More than 300 Muslim dynasties have ruled various portions of the Islamic world in the last 1300 years. Yet a Muslim could go into any of these sometimes isolated and sometimes warring states and find the same language, social order and laws "[108]

Some of the best-known Islamic dynasties include the Umayyad in Damascus, the Abbasid in Baghdad, the Fatimid and grandeur Mameluks in Egypt, the Umayyad Caliphate in Spain and the heritage of Andalusia, the Ottoman Empire and the Guarded Dominions. Therefore Islamic civilisation was a multi-racial civilisation that played a significant role in contributing to present-day modern civilisation and a real turning point in the advancement of humanity.

When one compares faith related civilisation, in the context of Judo-Christian civilisation to Islamic civilisation, there has been some profound difference in this aspect as the following quotation indicates: "Christianity had priesthood and no freedom of thought. The centuries in which the Christian Church was supreme are now referred to as the dark ages. Islam had no priesthood, it had freedom of thought and the ages when Islam prevailed in all its purity were ages of a singularly clear and brilliant light..."[109] Moreover, "According to M.M Pickthall the author of Cultural Side of Islam, the Muslims set out their search for learning in the name of God at a time when Christians (Christians in the west not Christianity) were destroying all the learning of ancients in the name of Christ. They have destroyed the library at Alexandria; they had murdered many philosophers including the beautiful Hypatia. Learning was for them a devil's snare beloved of pagans. They had no injunction to seek knowledge 'even though it was in China.' The priests publicly burned the manuscripts of Greek and Roman learning. The Western Romans had succumbed to barbarism. The Eastern Emperors kept their library and entertained some learned men, but within their palace walls...thus the Muslims saved the ancient learning from destruction and passed its treasures down to modern times" [110]

Of the three religions, Judaism, Christianity and Islam, the latter religion has contributed most to science. Islam also contributed significantly to art, literature architecture, navigation, geography, medicine, mathematics, philosophy and astrology. The Arabs also introduced to the Europeans universities, libraries, observatories, chess, cards and paper, which they in turn had taken from others. The Ottoman period of Islamic civilisation, which lasted into the twentieth century, was renowned for its tolerance and harmony amongst mixed races in the line of charities "organisations regulated entry to each craft or trade promotion in it and gave loans or grants to members who needed capital to open a shop or who had fallen on hard times."[111] The Turks introduced baths, lavatories, sanitations, basic hygiene and coffee; hence they are called 'Turkish bath', 'Turkish lavatory' and 'Turkish coffee'. The word coffee is said to have derived from the Cafa region of present-day Ethiopia. The Ethiopian coffee is called Mocha, which in turn originated from the Yemeni town of Mocha in the present day Republic of Yemen in the

Arabian Peninsula. At the turn of the nineteenth century the British French and the Dutch all use to get their coffee from Mocha. It was also at the palaces of the Othman rulers in Turkey that Britain and France use to send some of their service men to get training on how to be gentlemen. The graduation robe also originated from Islamic culture. The Europeans used to go to the universities of Andalusia. Upon their return they used to wear the Arab loose robe, which was an indication of their graduation. "...But one of Islam's greatest contributions lay in the encouragement that it gave to the spread of learning. The correspondence between learned men throughout the Arabic-speaking world resulted in the extensive collection and analysis of facts ... During the five centuries when Arabic was the international language of science, a man could live a full, useful, and rich life within the world of Islam, with no thought for the darkness outside."[112] Furthermore, "Students from France and England came to sit at the feet of Muslim, Christian and Jewish scholars to learn philosophy, science and medicine. What makes Andalusia so important in the history of civilisation is not just that life was lived nobly there but that it passed on to the Christian West the learning of both the Islamic and the Classical worlds."[113]

When the new Abbasid Dynasty took over from the Omayyad Caliph Marwan in 750, they too magnificently contributed to the progress and continuation of Islamic civilisation. It was the Umayyad who set up a postal service for correspondence and it was Ḥarūn al-Rashīd's son, Ma'mūn, of the Abbasid dynasty, who established the "House of Wisdom" in Baghdad, where the best minds met the challenge of human intellectual history. The collection, analysis and preservation of classical works took place. The spirit of questioning and reasoning flourished. Thinkers of other faiths included Arab Christians were also welcomed and participated "The philosophers of the Arabs, wrote over 250 works on optics, music, alchemy, astrology and philosophy. Rhazes, (al-Rāzī), a native of Rayy in Persia, wrote 141 works, including the first known clinical description of smallpox and measles"[114]. It was also during the Abbasid Dynasty that the tales of the Arabian Nights flourished. The Arabian Nights was very much the description of the then lives in

Baghdad and Cairo. However the tales also derive from other parts, such as India and Persia. "This collection of fairytales and popular romances forms the best known of Arabic writing outside the Arab world..."[115] In addition, the Fatimids of Egypt also extended the 'waqf', which is the Islamic charity system. It is a kind of endowment in which the revenues from a piece of property are solely assigned forever to a charitable and pious intention. It was under their rule that al-Azhar was accordingly built as a 'jâmi' i.e. a place of worship and learning as well, with considerable waqf endowment. During the two centuries of the Fatimid rule, the economy, social well being, law and order prevailed in Egypt. The Persian traveller Nasir-i-Khusraw in his Sifrnameh tells about how the then Cairo was in a high order. He mentions that prices were fixed and crime was curtailed to the extent that jewellers' shops were quite safe when left open. He refers all that to the fact that the state had followed the Islamic system

Moreover, Islamic architecture was substantial and extensive. It was the grandeur of the Mameluks in the 13-15 centuries in which Egyptian architecture flourished. The most famous hospital in Cairo was built. It consisted of three courtyards, two surrounded by cubicles for patients and the third by wards, library, lecture rooms, treatment and dispensary rooms. Like other Islamic hospitals, the patients were entertained with music and were comforted by Qur'ānic readings. Patients were not charged any fees. In effect, "In the words of Mr. Guy Le Strange: at that period of world history, Cordova, Cairo, Baghdad and Damascus were the only cities in the world which had police regulations (shurţa) and street lamps."[116] In the event "the art and the architecture of the Islamic world give ample evidence at the Muslim origin and creative genius."[117]

A lot has been borrowed from Islamic architecture. For instance "who would think that on entering a Gothic Church, one was looking at Islamic Mosque? ...In the late 12th century a revolutionary transformation occurred in the Christian architecture of Europe, when the Romanesque style was replaced by the Gothic. Round arches were no longer used, pointed arches came into favour, and ribbed vaults were introduced in place of groined vaults. Both these key features of Gothic were Islamic in origin. After 3000 years of the invariable employment of semi-circular arches, the Umayyad of Syria invented the pointed arches. The earliest building to have this distinction was the Dome of the Rock in Jerusalem, built only 70 years after the Hijra. As time went on, the separation of the two arches become wider and a more pronounced pointed form emerged. In the Ibn Tulun Mosque in Cairo (876), the mature arch appeared two centuries before it was introduced in Europe. The first in the Monastery of the Monte Cassino under Abbot Desiderius in 1066-71 by the builders from Amalfi, in southern Italy, who had trade links with the Muslim East, then to central France in the third church at Cluny in 1088-95. From there pointed arches were disseminated throughout Europe." [118]

Another elaborated culture of Islam that attracted the Christians was the trade of textiles. The industry of textile was profound in its fine and complicated patterns on silk and cotton embroidered with gold, compelling some churches in Europe, particularly in the Renaissance in Rome, to look for a cloth to wrap the Virgin Mary that has script from the Holy Qur`ān in Arabic, reading: lā 'Ilāh 'Ilā Allāh Muhammad Rasuululah (There is no god but God Muhammad is his messenger). Also the East has contributed to the west in clothing. Given that, the word damask originates from Damascus, muslin from Mosul baldachin from Baghdad, dimity from Damietta, fustian from Fustat, Taffeta from Persian word taftah satin from ar-zaytini. Others such as cotton and tabby were derived from the Spanish attabi via the French and Italian equivalent tabis. Other Italian textiles reveal their Persian origin. A century and a half ago while Europeans were discovering the pashmina loomwork of Kashmir, a number of Hindustani words like sash, pyjama and shawl (from the Persian word shal) passed into the English language... (See more on R.A. Jairasbhoy's book on oriental influences in western Art, pages 46, 47).

Other areas where Islamic civilisation contributed include democracy and the judiciary systems elaborated by 'Umar bin al-Khaṭāb. It is argued, for instance, "the struggle for democracy in the sense of equality did not begin with the importation of the Universal Declaration of Human Rights, which is western ...It began in the first centuries of Islam with the Kharijite sect..."[119] The Kharijites were regarded as those "who quit" and acknowledged the right of the community to choose its own head and to depose him for wrongdoing.

It has been claimed in accordance with Professor Abdalla El-Tayib, scholar from the Sudan, through his former student Mohammed Jallal (who is a Sudanese Journalist and writer), that the word jury is derived from the Arabic word *shūrī*, which is the adjective from *shūrāh*. In Andalusia, the Muslim judges used to have a committee of counselling aides whose responsibility was to decide the case verdict. The judge was responsible for deciding the sentence. Therefore, the confusion of the word *sūra* with the Latin word *Jurare*, to swear, happened as those counselling aides were made to swear before trials. They took the system, dropping *surie* because it is alien to the Latin interpretation.

Most civilisations have their spiritual and material aspects. Under the Islamic civilisation therefore, the arts of literature poetry, fashion and music flourished. Mir Ziryab, who was Irani, won a musical contest in Baghdad; he then moved to Cordoba and started an academy of music, then became an arbiter of fashion. "It was to Cordoba, not to Paris, that the ladies of Christian kingdoms of Navarre and Aragon sent for their new dresses. At a time when London could not boast a single street-lamp, the streets in the cities of Andalusia were paved and lit. The houses had marble balconies for the summer and hot-air ducts under the mosaic floors for the winter. They were surrounded by gardens adorned with pools and artificial cascades and by orchards of peaches and pomegranates."[120]

At the time when the local capital of the Umayyad caliphate was Qayrawan in Tunisia, it was the group led by Ṭāriq Ibn Ziyād who conquered Spain in 711 and the present day Gibraltar got its name from the Muslim leader Ṭāriq; Its Arabic name Jabal Ṭāriq (Mount of Tariq).

Some of the best-known Muslims who contributed to world civilisation in different fields include the following: Ibn Khaldūn, whose most famous work is the "Muqaddamah" (introduction to history), in which he discussed historical methods and the criteria for distinguishing historic truth from error. It is considered one of the most phenomenal works on the philosophy of history ever written. He said, "He who finds a new path is a pathfinder, even if the trail is to be found again by others and he who walks far ahead of his contemporaries is a leader, even though centuries pass before he is recognised as such." Ibn Khaldūn was also the father of sociology and the science of history. (See more on Ibn Khaldūn, historian and philosopher in Melissa Snell's "Guide to Medieval History"). Ibn an-Nafīs 'Ala ad-Din Abu-l-Hasan (610-687/1213-1288) was born in Damascus and was a physician who worked in Cairo at the Nāsrī and Mansūrī hospitals, making remarkable contributions to medicine (The institution of care for the sick at hospitals was established in the first centuries of Islamic civilisation.). Ibn Baytar Abu Muhammad 'Abd Allāh ibn Ahmad Diya' ad-Din (d.646/1248) was botanist born in Malaga who wrote the greatest compilation of medicinal plants made before modern times, the Khitāb al-Jāmi' fi-l-Adwiyah al-Mufradah. It contains 1,400 entries including many plants never before recorded, and cites a number of Latin and Greek authors. Al Khuwārizmī, Abu J'afar Muhammud, B. Mūsa, was a mathematician, astronomer and geographer who utilised the Arabic language. He lived in the first half of the 3rd /9th century (c184-c232/800-47). He worked in the Bayt al-Hikma of Baghdad during the Caliphate of al M'amūn. His works are well known since many of them were translated into Latin in Spain and exercised a powerful influence on the development of medieval thought. His algebra called al-Mukhtasar if his al-diabr wa al muqkābala (ed. with Eng. tr. F. Rosen, the algebra of ... London 1831, repr. New York 1969 ed. Ali Mustafi Musharrafa and M - Mursl; Ahmed, Cairo 1939) ...in this way, there was introduced into Europe a science completely unknown till then and with it a terminology which was still capable of growth but already completely developed. Khwārazmī's work, which had a great influence on the birth of western science, was his Zidji al-Sindhird, astronomical tables translated into Latin by Adelard of Bath. They also used Egyptian fractions, those with 1 as the numerator and from which one can obtain the others by means of addition (e.g. $1/3 + 1/15 = 2/5$; $\frac{1}{4} + 1/28 = 2/7$). This type of fraction already appears in the Rhind papyrus and developed over the ancient and mediaeval periods, especially when the system of Qur`ānic inheritance rules gave rise to the `ilm al-farā`id´ and made necessary the perfecting of arithmetical operations using fractions. The system, by now completely developed, was introduced to Europe through the intermediary of various Spanish versions and through that of Fibonacci". Ib Zuhar, Abu Marwān 'Abd al- Malik (d. 557/1162) was one of the great Arab physicians called Avonzoar in medical Europe, where his work was very influential. He also knew Ibn Rushd and Ibn Tufayl. His works on medicine, which demonstrated a good knowledge of anatomy, were translated first into Hebrew and then into Latin. Ibn Khalliqān, Abu -l-'Abbās Ahmed (608-68/1211-1282) was a biographer born in Iraq. His book Wafayāt al-A'yān, is one of the most important works of reference, along with those of al-Waqidī, for biographical information on more than 800 of the great men up to his time (Encyclopaedia of Islam New Editions Leiden, PPs, 1070, 1071, 933, 932, 927, 170, 171, 176, 177). Furthermore, King Roger II of the Normans sponsored al-'Idrīsī (author of Geography of the World). Hence the Normans continued to use Arabic to benefit the knowledge it entailed. This list is not exhaustive!

As late as 7 June 2004, the Bodleian Library in Oxford displayed for the first time an Arabic manuscript called The Kitāb Gharā'ib al-Funūn wa-Mulāh al-'Uyūn (The book of Curiosities of Science and Marvels of the Eye). The book reflects the achievements of the classical age of Islamic civilisation. It includes a new array of medieval maps. Lesley Forbes, keeper of oriental collections at the library said: "…for example, the rectangular world map in the book of curiosity (Gharā'ib al-Funūn) is of a type previously completely unknown, and we believe, unique to this manuscript. There is a rare illustrated discourse on comets and a unique illustrated guide to stars used in navigation and weather prediction". This book also shows a map of British Isles with Arabic name "Angle-terre", which these researches believe is the earliest depiction in connection with that name. According to Jeremy Johns of Wolfson College, one of two scholars in charge of the exhibition, "the treatise is extraordinarily important for the history of science."[121]

Therefore, whilst the works of the Renaissance have been sharply articulated, detailed and praised, the achievements of the Muslim scholars from whom the west gained so much are seldom remembered.

So, to suggest that western civilisation is based on Greek civilisation is to be in a state of structural amnesia, as the anthropologists say when the natives select what to remember and what not. The Greek civilisation predominantly derived from Egyptian civilisation. Case in point: "Greek architects drew on the experience of the Egyptians in achieving their own mastery in-working, and in use of the column. In the sphere of art, the influence of Egypt was far-reaching. A whole repertory of typically Egyptian motifs and symbols such as the key of life, the sphinx, the winged disc and the lotus were adopted by the Phoenicians and spread throughout the Mediterranean world. Some are still popular today. The Egyptian style of depicting human and animal figures was widely imitated and it influenced early Greek sculpture and vase painting; the early statues of Greek gods and heroes have the same fixed stare and the advanced left foot that are typical of the classical tradition in Egypt "[122]

In short, much of what the classical world called the 'secret wisdom' of Egyptians was passed on to the Greeks. Even the 365-day calendar still used today is claimed to be of Egyptian origin "They dated their year from the appearance of the star Sirius just before the Nile's annual floods and divided it into 12 months."[123] "The name of the Bible derives from the Lebanese town of Bybols, which was a chief market"[124]. Two hundred years ago Napoleon broke the flat nose of Sphinx in Egypt at the Pyramids, as he might have had difficulty accepting that the Egyptian civilisation was indeed a black people's civilisation.

In post-modern times many scientists, including medical doctors seem to embrace Islam in the context of knowledge and science. One example of Islam in the history of science is the area of anatomy and embryology. Professor Emeritus Keith L. Moore, who in 1984 received the most distinguished award presented in the field of anatomy in Canada, articulated his observation about the subject matter. In 1981, during the Seventh Medical Conference in Dammam, he said the following: "Because the staging of human embryos is complex, owing to the continuous process of change development, it is proposed that a new system of classification could be developed using the terms mentioned in the Qur`ān and Sunnah. (What Muhammad said, did or approved). The proposed system is simple, comprehensive and conforms to present embryological knowledge. The intensive studies of the Qur`ān and Hadeeth in the last four years have revealed a system for classifying human embryos that is amazing since it was recorded in the seventh century A.D." [125] Consequently Professor Moore was asked the following question: "Does this mean that you believe that the Qur`ān is the word of God?" He replied, "I find no difficulty in accepting this," and added, "The only reasonable conclusion is: These descriptions were revealed to Muhammad from God. He could not have known such details because he was an illiterate man with absolutely no scientific training."[126]

Furthermore, on many occasions modern geology and the science of modern cosmology have also confirmed the reality of the Qur`ānic verses. Dr. Alfred Kroner, who is one of the world's renowned geologists, commented that things like 'origin of the universe', which scientists only found out within the last few years, with very complicated and advanced technological methods, are already explained in the Qur`ān."[127]

Therefore, the proposition that Islam has not contributed to modernity or contemporary western science is basically a fallacy. That Islam is irrelevant to post modernity is equally incorrect. The point is that many Muslims, "At certain period of their history, they began to turn to their backs upon a part of what had been enjoyed (sic) to them, they discarded half the Shariah – the part which ordered them to seek knowledge and education, and to study God's creation. And the Christians of the West about the same time began to set according to that portion of Shariah which (sic) the Muslims were discarding, and so advanced [in certain areas] in spite of all the anathemas of their priesthood. The reason why it was ordained that there should be no priesthood in Islam is because ecclesiasticism is an enemy to human progress, …the aim is shown in the Qur'ān to be the progress and liberation of humanity..." [128].

Therefore, within the parameters of comparative religion, in particular Judaism, Christianity and Islam, the latter is chronologically and intellectually the most modern whilst it entails a provision that guides one's every day way of life, it also contains cultivated dimensions of scholarship in the universe (not only the other life, as it is often portrayed) that sharpens the knowledge of the universe in its entirety.

The contemporary projection of Judaic Christian western civilisation hegemony is rarely adequate, whilst the west's borrowing of knowledge from the Muslims is immensely detailed and recorded.

In terms of divergences and convergences between religions, Judaism, Christianity and Islam are, as one is aware, complementary. Muslims do believe both Judaism and Christianity, but certainly not when it comes to certain details, including the issues between the Roman Catholics and the Protestants and many others, such as the belief that "Jesus died for the sins of the world and that Jesus went to hell for three days" [129]. Whilst both religions (Islam and Christianity) agree the miraculous birth of Jesus, they differ in interpretation for instance.

Whilst the Holy Qur'ān confirms the miraculous birth of Jesus as follows in answer to her logical question: "O my Lord! How shall I have a son when no man hath touched me?" The Angels say in reply: "Even so: Allah createth what He willeth; when He hath decreed a plan, He but saith to it "Be" and it is!" (Holly Qur'ān 3:4)". Moreover, "to believe [that] Jesus was the Messiah and the Son of God...the Jewish priests regarded this as blasphemous" [130]. Also "In many places the Jews were resented, for most Christians held them responsible for the death of Christ. They were confined to ghettos and forbidden to own land or to practice (sic) trade..." [131]

Furthermore, the following quotation indicates that Moses and Muhammad were accepted as prophets by their people in their lifetime: "No doubt the Jews gave endless trouble to Moses and they murmured in the wilderness, but as nation as a whole, they acknowledged that Moses was a Messenger of God sent to them. The Arabs too made Muhammad's life impossible. He suffered very badly at their hands. After 13 years of preaching in Mecca, he had to emigrate from the city of his birth. But before his demise, the Arab nation as a whole accepted him as the Messenger of Allah. [However], ... according to the Bible - 'He (Jesus) came unto his own, but his own received him not.'(John 1:11) and even today, after two thousand years, his people - the Jews, as a whole, have rejected him,"[132]

However, Jesus, his mother Mary, Moses and rest of those Islam lists as Prophets are well-mentioned in the Qur`ān. Whilst Islam believes both religions, it encompasses and extends from there. For example George Bemard Shaw, author of the book, "The Genuine Islam Vol.1, no. 81936." stated: "I have studied him - the wonderful man - and in my opinion far from being an anti-Christ, he (Prophet Muhammad) must be called the saviour of humanity"[133]. Moreover, a Hindu scholar, Diwan Chand Shama in his book entitled "The Prophets of the East" Calcutta 1935, wrote: "Muhammad was the soul of kindness, and his influence was felt and never forgotten by those around him."[134] Also, in the Encyclopaedia Britannica, 11th edition, it is stated that: "Mohamed was the most successful of all religious personalities."[135]

Of the Qur'ān, there is no old or new version and millions learn it by heart. Muslim scholars debate and discuss the embodied knowledge. The grand muftis and learned men are able to interpret and explain in detail. Throughout the emergence of Islam, no one was successful in modifying the Qur'ān; neither an eloquent poet nor an exuberant author managed to change any verse in the Qur'ān.

Nonetheless, the commonality amongst religions on good deeds is seldom scarce. It is worth noting that almost all religions, including the Baha and Hindu, are in convergence when it comes to morals and values, not to mention decency and harmony. All promote peace and denounce violence. For instance, an ethic that has been variously repeated in all the great religions is the teaching that we should treat others as we ourselves would wish to be treated.

Islam as a religion calls for justice to all and is very much a religion of mercy based on merit. In the Qur'ān, God says: "God does not forbid you from showing kindness and dealing justly with those who have not fought you about religion and have not driven you out of your homes. God loves just dealers" (Qur'ān, 60:8). Like Judaism and Christianity, Islam does not meddle with Darwinians and Freudians. The ethos of most religions does not accept the hegemony of masculinity, incest, etc. and, unlike politicians and political doctrines, most religious theologies are not subject to revision, changes and amendments in order to manage the apparatus of the ever-changing world. Instead, the existing version is studied continually with the human effort of attempting to understand and conceptualise embedded knowledge. Generally speaking, therefore, to conform or to reject and to apprehend religious teachings is basically humanistic in all spheres and across religions.

To synthesise the issues and the problems discussed above, there should be a clear definition and separation between secularism and monotheism. Secular thoughts are endowed with reason, convincing, logical, aided by modern science and wrapped with the visible chain of the human mind, in contrast with the divine theologies enacted beyond the reach of human reasoning. In the west, the interplay between Christianity on one hand and modern science on the other hand have been mistakenly intertwined recently, as if the achievements of science are part of a modern religion of Christ in the west. It should be underlined that the secularists look to science as an alternative to religion changing the institutions of western governments and having a profound impact on the structure of western society. Consequently, the two could not mitigate each other and they differed in substance. The human intellectual power has been cultivated through scholars of different fields. For that, opting for science has been considered as enlightenment and progressiveness, having few attributes with metaphysical moral dimensions. In effect, a strong sense of judiciary and fair trial procedures has been engaged to replace the persecutions, among other achievements of the time, in Europe. In the process of engaging scientific and philosophical scholarships, the west, in particular Europe has tremendously benefited from the Islamic civilisation that was then rich. Not only did Islam conceptualise science, but Muslim scholars were also very advanced. Unlike other religions, "At the same time Islam was providing the chief intellectual stimulus to the west it was spreading rapidly through the Indian sub-continent, Russia, China and Indonesia. United by the holy language, Arabic and by the five simple precepts which are observed by the true believers, it proved capable of adjusting its political and cultural forms to the most diverse tribes and peoples. No other religion - even Christianity when it harvested the gentile fellow travellers of the Synagogues of the Diaspora - has ever spread so rapidly and gained so many adherents as Islam in its first two centuries"[136] Moreover, "Under the Abbasid caliphs, there were Nestorians, Melchite and Jewish communities - all three enjoying greater toleration than under the Byzantine state-church, ...Although Muslims and Christians were officially at each others' throats ...political and economic divisions often cut along other than faith lines. ...Not until the Crusades did a somewhat united Christendom face a somewhat united Islam, and even there the western Christians pillaged the capital of Eastern Orthodoxy and the rulers of the Crusader Kingdoms speedily sought alliance with different Muslim emirs to strengthen their hand against each other."[137]

However," In most fields of knowledge the Muslims' civilisation was far more advanced than Christendom... "[138]. Hence Europe, made through the industrial age and Renaissance, calumniated in the slave trade that has been described as the most inhuman act in the history of mankind, and there is great difference between slaves and slave trade in the form of human shipment of the sort.

Nevertheless, what combined liberal minds of different faiths, regardless of their social background and nationalities, has been the shift from religious dogmatism and the centre point has been the maintenance of mutual respect, human dignity, civil liberty, morals and the universal virtues of friendship, understanding of diversity, enhancement of coexistence and curtailment of the language of conflict. In some cases nationalism and patriotism have been considered as backwardness. Therefore sophistications and fines were synonymous with cross-culture sensitivities. To appreciate the beauty and the taste of diverse cultures and environments is to be regarded as enriched.

In other words, the revisionism of religious battles of old, within or between faiths, is displaying an exhaustion of modernity and a reversal of civilisation; a civilisation based on combustion and continuity, in which no group has the monopoly or righteous claim for its totality. It is a dangerous venture of backwardness to evoke religious paradigms and faith-based confrontations in the twenty-first century.

It should not be difficult to grasp the difference between contrasting ideologies, e.g. capitalism vis-à-vis communism, and that of faith confrontation. To pick Islam as the new enemy in the place of the then Warsaw Pact is a rather obscure venture, partly because there is no Islamic empire to overthrow, as was the case during the Ottoman reign. Ironically, the Turkish republic is now aiming to be part of Europe, has a treaty of friendship with Israel and is a member of NATO. There have been no organised Islamic military forces since Ottoman times, partly because there is no clarity of who the combating forces are. Is it Muslims against Christians, the USA, the west, capitalism or secularism and where is the power base of this Muslim menace? The enemy is not only invisible but the topography is also blurred, taking into account the geographical and ethnic diversification of Muslims around the globe. In short, the more anti-Islamic rhetoric propagates, the thinner the case appears and the more exposed anti-Muslims become. Therefore such an animosity search is not only a long haul but, indeed, a lost cause.

6. Chapter Six

Islam has been portrayed as religion that negates women's rights. Some of the western media as well as politicians seem to suggest that indeed Islam oppresses women. Therefore it is worth articulating briefly women's rights in different societies. And the impressive array of rights that Islam gives to women as religion.

6.1 Does Islam Oppress Women?

According to Abdulrahman A.Sheeha, the author of "Woman in the Shade of Islam" and an authority on the subject matter: "…There is not a single law, system or regulation that preserves, maintains and protects women's rights as much as Islam does, whether in the past or in modern times."[139] In addition to that, the famous French thinker Gustave Le Bond wrote the following in his book, "The Arab Civilisation" (in p488): "Islamic virtuous deeds are not limited to honouring and respecting women, but rather, we can add that Islam is the first religion to honour and respect. We can easily prove this by illustrating that all religions and nations prior to the advent of Islam caused much harm and insult to women." In p497 he added: "Matrimonial rights which have been stated and illustrated in the Glorious Qur`ān and by the interpreters of the meaning of the Glorious Qur`ān are far better than European matrimonial rights for both husband and wife" 140 . "As late as 1586, there was a conference held in France to decide whether woman was to be considered a human being or not! After lengthy discussions, the people who attended the conference came to a conclusion that: 'woman is a human being but she is created to serve man'…"[141] Centuries before that there were women heads of state in certain quarters of the then Muslim world. Furthermore, long before the times when the then English laws permitted a man to sell his wife, the famous Taj Mahal existed. The Moghul Emperor Shah Jahan built that mausoleum in the memory of his beloved wife. Muslims ruled in India for 900 years and The Taj Mahal took twenty years to finish.

In the earlier Christian societies, priests considered women as the cause of "original sin" and regarded a physical relationship between man and woman even in marriage "filthy", even if it was officially performed within a legitimate marriage contract.[142] Women in the old Jewish Society were described as follows (in the Old Testament 7:25-26): "Both my heart and I searched and sought wisdom and good judgment, to know that evil (acts) are nothing but ignorance and stupidity, foolishness and madness. I found that more better (sic) the death is women as she is a net, her heart is a trap and here hands are shackles (or handcuffs)"[143]

In the Hindu society, women were forbidden to live after the death of their husbands and were burned in the same funeral pyre with the deceased husband. This custom was outlawed as late as the end of the 17th century, thus dismaying Hindu religious leaders who wanted to continue such practices. In certain parts of India women were brought to sacrifice to Hindu gods. Some Hindu laws declare that: "The predestined patience, the blow wind or tornadoes, death, hellfire, poison, snakes and fire are no less worst (sic) than woman (the Female)."[144]

The position and the status of women in the Chinese society was very much the same as that of pagan pre-Islamic Arab society and a Chinese proverb says, "Listen to your wife, but never believe what she says".

The issue of polygamy is too often attributed to Islam, even though Islam inherited it from the other religions of the Book prior to the Prophet Muhammad, peace be upon him.

Case in point: Both the Old Testament, and the New Testament include the list of the Divine Books that stated the practice and legalised plural marriages. "The Prophet Abraham had two wives and Jacob had four wives. The Old Testament stated that the Prophet David had ninety-nine wives. It also stated that Prophet Solomon had seven hundred wives who were free noble women and three hundred other wives who were slave women. [145]

At present, there are many polytheist communities that practice polygamy. Some argue that plural marriages are as old as the

119

history of mankind itself. Whilst modernity and secularism advocated discarding polygamy, the desire of male preference for more then one wife/women has not been removed. Indeed, there are mistresses and girlfriends who would not have the same rights as wives. It is fair for women of all faiths to raise the question of polygamy. It is equally human for some to accept the religious and traditional explanations and some to reject them. As late as 1964, a decree from Oxford University was passed to declare equality between female and male students.

As for women's equal rights with men, in the context of Catholicism or Judaism, modifications of such sorts have been almost second to none. For instance, in the three main strands of Judaism, Orthodox, Conservative and Reform. The Orthodox argue that they are the correct version of the Judaic faith and up to the present men and women sit separately in the synagogue and women have no right to approach the ark. In some sects, such as the Aguna in Judaism, a husband can deny a woman divorce and she will not be able to remarry without the divorce, like the Rabbi in Kabul who refuses to divorce his wife in Israel and she cannot remarry. In Catholicism, there is no right of divorce and women are very much regarded as subservient to men in many ways. Moreover, it is stated in the Genesis 3:16 " Unto the women he said, I will greatly multiply thy sorrow and thy conception; in sorrow thou shalt bring forth children and thy desire shall be thy husband and he shall rule over thee." The Qur`ān states 4:19: "If you dislike them, it may be that you dislike one thing and Allah brings through it a great deal of good."[146] Verse 30:21 states: "Among His signs is this, that He created for you wives from among yourselves, that you may find repose in them and He has put between you affection and mercy. Verily, in that are indeed signs for people who reflect," [147] Islam urges men to treat their wives kindly, gently and with a caring and sharing attitude. The Apostle of Allah was reported as saying, "The most complete believers in terms of faith are those who possess the best morals. The best of you are those best to their wives".[148]. Where women and men are different in terms of mental, physical, psychological and emotional abilities and strengths, the Qur`ān provides ample knowledge and explanations of reasons for gender differences, commonalities and the applications of rules and regulations are accommodating to one's circumstances and situations. Variations of one's abilities and position are considered at all times (And if you are a believer, Allah knows the best). It is stated in the Glorious Qur'ān 49:13: "O mankind, we have created you from a male and a female and made you into nations and tribes, that you may know one another. Verily, the most honourable of you in the sight of Allah is the believer who has taqwa (i.e. piety and righteousness) and loves Allah most. Verily, Allah is All-Knowing. All-Aware." [149]

One of the issues that need to be understood is the factual limitation on human freedoms and liberties and the aspects of its totality in relation to law, decency and human dignity. The guidance to those values and morals is what separates humans from other animals, in particular the Haywan–al-muftaris (wild animals). So, whilst liberty, equality and freedom are of major importance to human development as well as one's human rights, the misuse and abuse of those rights is equally detrimental. Indeed, that is why societies practise and safeguard laws and constitutions, whether they are customary, religious or otherwise. The models of those rules and regulations do vary from one country, nation or group within a nation. It is worth noting the comments made by Helesian Stanbery, who is an American women journalist and broadcaster for over twenty years and who visited numerous Islamic countries. She said the following: "The Arab-Islamic society …must continue to protect its traditions that restrict both its males and females to a certain and reasonable degree…First and foremost, the most strict restrictions and limitations are on absolute sexual freedom that truly threatens both the society and the family in Europe and the United States…Because we have suffered from it in the USA. The American society has become sophisticated, full of all forms and terms of sexual freedom. The victims of sexual freedom and coeducation are filling the prisons, sidewalks (sic) bars. The (false) freedom which we have granted to our young females and daughters has turned them to drugs, crime and white slavery …and all other types of "freedom" in the European and American societies have threatened the family and shaken moral values and ethics." [150]

In fairness, however, the Arabs and other Muslim societies are not maleka (Angels) either, but whilst to sin and to be rampant is human, to normalise indecency in the name of liberation and freedom is questionable. "Islam has forbidden women from being publicly indecent, sexually provocative...this is a freedom from which the male in Islam, equally as well has been stripped..."[151] Moreover, "Islam has entitled women to the same rights insofar as chastity, integrity and personal honour and respect are concerned, and persons who falsely accuses any women with immoral acts or indecency shall be publicly punished similar to the treatment of man."[152]

Islam is a meritocracy and women do not change their family names once married, unlike the west, where women's surnames are subject to change in accordance to those of their husbands.

Despite the contentious debates however, Muslim women ruled and reigned as sovereigns, in Africa, Asia, the Middle East and Europe. Women also engage in politics, business and battles.

6.2 Cases in Point.

Sultan Radiyy Bint Shams al Din and Shajarat al- Durr, who were both Turks, played a significant role in the Islamic empire of the time. Sultan Radiyy Bint Shams al Din took power in Delhi in 634 / 1236. Shajarat al- Durr mounted the throne of Egypt 648 / 1250. "She brought the Muslims a victory which the French remember well, because she routed their army during the Crusades and captured their king, Louis..."[153]

During the 14th and 15th centuries, from 714/1336 to 814/1411, Tindu ruled Iraq during the Jallarid dynasty.

In Iran, Absh Khatun ruled the country from 662/1263 to 686/1287. She was the ninth sovereign of the Persian dynasty for a quarter of a century.

Women also governed the Muslims of Maldives for 40 years. The first Sultana was Rehendhi Khadija then Sultana Myriam and was succeeded by Sultan Fatima who was the daughter of Sultana Myriam and ruled that country from 790/1388

In Indonesia, four princesses succeeded each other in the second half of the seventh century, from 1641 to 1699 and they were: Sultana Tadj al-Alam, Sultan Nur al-Alam, Inayat Shah and Kamalat Shah.

In Yemen there were Malika Asma and Malika Arwa, who exercised power in the San'a at during the eleventh century. Araw held power for almost 50 years. "She directed the affairs of the state and planned war strategies until she died in 484/1090."[154]

In Morocco there was 'A'isha al- Hurra, known to the Spaniards by the name Sultana Madre de Boabdil. She won the admiration of her enemies at the time of Muslim debacle "According to Abdallah Inan, an expert on the fall of Granada,… she played a prominent role in Muslim history …and the Spanish documents revealed that she was a remarkable leader who took heroic actions at tragic moment; he calls her one of the most noble and fascinating [personage] of our history…"[155] Sayyida al- Hurra, also Moroccan of Andalusia origin, who was the governor of a Tetouan, exercised power for more than 30 years 916/1510 to 949/1542. "…The Spaniards and the Portuguese maintained close relations with her as the responsible naval power in the region, and negotiated with her for the liberation of their prisoners."[156]

In Egypt, one of the heads of the Fatimid dynasty was Queen Sitt al- Mulk Who organised the disappearance of her brother who ordered women to stay in their homes and she took power in 411/1021.

Trimmingham noted that the "… position of women in Southern Arabia and the Cushities whom they coalesced with is high."[157]

However, even during those times some men were not pleased with women's leadership. For instance, during the Fatimid dynasty in Egypt, some Ulama (religious leaders) challenged female leadership and passed decrees occasionally. But the claim that Islam negates women's position in politics, businesses or decision-making processes as well as the freedom to express their view in public is very much incoherent. Muslim women ruled and reigned and it hasn't been dull to engage the debate on sex equities amongst scholars, including religious scientists and experts as well as laymen. The Prophet Muhammad's wife (peace be upon him), Khadija was a business woman. She employed the prophet and, not only was she older than him, but she proposed to him. It is also interesting to note Dr Mohammad Akram Nadwi, a research fellow at Centre of Islamic Studies in Oxford about his work on female scholars of *Hadith* in Islam. Dr Akram's study provides biographical details of the narrations of over 8,000 female scholars of *Hadith*. The Muslim women of the time took keen interest in almost all academic disciplines and made significant and outstanding contributions. "There has been no dispute among scholars regarding the equality of men and women in their capabilities and responsibilities in receiving and imparting knowledge, even as Muslim societies have sometimes been reluctant or even opposed to seeing these responsibilities fulfilled." For instance, an expert on language was Safiyah bint al-Murtada b. al-Mufaddal (d. 771 A.H). She wrote a number of books. Al Suyuti has narrated the celebrated Arabic dictionary al-Qamus from six women; Asiyah bint Jarullah b. Salih al-Tabri, Safiyyah bint Yaqut al-Makkiyyah, Ruqayyah bint Abd al-Qawi b. Muhammad al-Bijadi, Umm Hababah bint Ahmad b. Musa al Shuwayki, Kamaliyyah bint Ahmad b. Muhammad b. Nasir al-Makki and Umm al- Fadl Hajir bint Sharaf al- Maqdisi

In today's Muslim world women's position in various sectors of the state and society differs from one country to another. In other words, there is no uniformity. In practice, most countries are often inclined to devolve traditional mechanisms, whilst the Sharia practices remain applicable but are not always operational or invoked properly.

In the event, to empower and to enable women to participate in nation-building and state affairs differs from one country to another. For instance, whilst in Switzerland there are/were Muslim women ambassadors representing their missions; those of Malaysia, Libya, Egypt, Kenya and Somalia, in Saudi Arabia a lot has been discussed about women driving. Furthermore, in the wider Muslim world women are not docile about taking part in issues that affect their lives. Formally or informally, they exercise their power of influence in both domestic and state affairs, despite the fact that they still are very much in the minority when it comes to decision-making. Nevertheless there are Muslim women who are judges, ministers, directors, in the army and in the police, pilots, journalists, news presenters, musicians, singers, scientists, professors, writers, bankers, lawyers, artists, ballet dancers and so on. In places like Indonesia, Turkey and Pakistan, women held higher positions before certain European countries enabled to their women to gain such high positions. Therefore, the rhetoric that Muslim women are in urgent need to be liberated is very much based on a fallacy. There are improvements to be made yes, but a significant distinction should be made between raising the universally unequal nature of the rights of men and women, the lack of equity in a wider spectrum, and that of the religious manifestation and its embodied literature.

The reality is that, in every society around the globe, women encounter segregation in almost every context. It has been the case that the United Nations, as well as individual countries and agencies, continue to tackle women's problems. Despite those activities in attempting to maximise women's participation in political and social decision-making, these aspirations have not materialised, hence the political socio-economic gap between the sexes remains huge. The feminist movements in the west are still struggling to be heard. Child and domestic servility are still very much considered female zones of responsibility. Furthermore, women are ominously discriminated against in most office jobs, specifically positions regarded as male-oriented domains. It is worthy to note how a British woman working in the City of London has been forced to leave her job because she encountered sexism and was bullied by her male colleagues.

The following quotation indicates here predicament: "A city banker was driven out of her job by a campaign of bullying and sexual harassment (by) male colleagues, an employment tribunal heard yesterday. Carina Coleman, ...the only women working at the bank and the highest paid employee said she was called a dog, bitch and tethered goat by her chief tormenter. He mocked the size of her breasts and suggested a red light be fitted in their open-plan office to tell her colleagues when she was having periods, the tribunal was told. She said she was excluded from key meetings despite being head of the corporate finance and investment department." Then, "She claimed that she went sick, suffered from depression-related illness and resigned."[158]

It should be made clear that violence against women is a universal problem, which must be globally condemned, as was recognised at the International Women's Conference in Beijing in September, 1995. Therefore, the perception that women in Asia, Arabia or Africa suffer more violations than women in the west may not necessarily be the case. Such attempts are often considered disproportionate and intensely political (especially when used out of context).

For example, in the US, according to this quotation: "Every day four women die in this country as a result of domestic violence, the euphemism for murders and assaults by husbands and boy friends. That's approximately 1,400 women a year, according to the FBI. The number of women who have been murdered by their intimate partners is greater than the number of soldiers killed in the Vietnam War ...Battering, although only 572,000 reports of assault by intimates are officially reported to federal officials each year, the most conservative estimates indicate two to four million women of all races and classes are battered each year. At least 170,000 of those violent incidents are serious enough to require hospitalisation, emergency room care or doctor's attention...Sexual assault. Every year approximately 132,000 women report that they have been victims of rape or attempted rape, and more than half of them knew their attackers. It's estimated that two to six times that many women are raped, but do not report it. Every year, 1.2 million women are forcibly raped by their current or former male partners, some more than once." [159] It has been reported that in Afghanistan and in Iraq over 112 American women claimed that their colleagues in the army raped them.

Furthermore, scientists, academics and theologians in the west still maintain a strong argument regarding sexual mainstreaming and the inequalities between men and women in certain aspects of life. For instance, it has been reported that, "A brain scanning technology does show real physiological differences. The brain is a sex organ," said Dr. Sandra Witelson, a leading Canadian neurosurgeon. "Testosterone floods the male foetus and produces changes in its neural wiring. Thus boys and girls react to the world in different ways. Men can better separate cognitive and emotional issues. Men can push a painful emotional experience - an ill son or daughter for example - to the back of their minds when they come to work," said Witelson. "A woman finds that more difficult. As a result, their cognitive performance can be affected, giving women a disadvantage, particularly in important, stressful jobs. On the other hand, this ability to combine cognitive and emotional thinking makes women far more important to families and communities."[160] Similarly, a Harvard president, Larry Summers, asked the question: "Why can't women be more like a man?" "That", led the article entitled Women's Place, "is not Harvard. That mentions that women are behind in science and maths."[161]

Furthermore, in the UK, a major study reveals a catalogue of sexist, insults, hostility and boorish behaviour despite the influx of women MPs. "Bullied, patronised and abused women MPs revealed the truth about life inside Westminster ...When Gillian Shephard arrived in the House of Commons as a new Tory MP in 1987 she was confused to find herself and her fellow women MPs being called Betty. 'There was a conservative MP who called us all Betty' she recalls 'and when I said, 'look you know my name isn't Betty'; he said 'Ah, but you're all the same so I call you all Betty'...More than 15 years later with a big increase in the number of women MPs life has moved on – but only a little... The study was overseen by Joni Lovenduski of Birkbeck College. More then 100 hours of tapes of interviews with women

MP's is lodged in the British Library. The interviews show how even after the great influx of women in 1997-120 (sic) of them in total, female MPs were expected to stick to traditional "women issues", such us health and education. Several complained of put-downs they experienced when stepping on to the male territory of defence. A typical recollection is from Glenda Jackson who says that while she was speaking on defence a Tory MP called out: "Stick to what you know Glenda". When Labour's Dari Taylor resigned from the defence select committee – one of only two women on it the chairman, Bruce George, stood up and said: 'well, I have to make this announcement: one down one to go'..." [162]

Moreover, the late Pope John Paul gave a warning and attacked feminist ideologies, which assert that men and women are fundamentally the same. According to a leaked extract, the document accuses feminists of 'blurring the biological difference between men and women. The Vatican's sights are trained in particular on the view that, whilst people's sex is anatomically determined, their sexual identities and roles are entirely the product of conditioning. In a letter to bishops on the participation of men and women in the church and the world, the [then] Pope's chief theological spokesman, then German Cardinal Joseph Ratzinger (now Pope Benedict XVI) stressed, as the pontiff had done on several occasions, that the Book of Genesis is unambiguous on this point. [163]

Inconsistently, a lot has been said about Islamic fundamentalists who order women to wear the veil, but less has been mentioned when it comes to actions such as the works of western industry that promote women strippers, pornography, modelling, dieting and plastic surgery. Critics argue that extensions of such actions are considered abusive to women's rights and dignity.

Furthermore, as much as female circumcision is bad and is considered a traditionally harmful practice, nothing to do with Islam, nevertheless equal attention has not been paid to what some women in the north go through in the name of beauty by turning to plastic surgery on different parts of their bodies at different ages. One may counter-argue that those women may have willingly chosen to seek plastic surgery unlike the youngsters in families, but the reality behind all is the universal conditioning of women's bodies to conform to what some argue is a man's world. Many women from the south regard such a matter as horrific. Therefore, it seems that one needs to be careful in one's attitude towards other cultures. Obviously, what is all right in one place may not be necessarily comprehendible in another place.

To sum up: To suggest that Islam is a religion that oppresses women is either lacking sufficient knowledge of Islam or in a position of ultra motives or selective bias against Islam or all three. There is sufficient evidence to suggest that Islam gives more rights to women than any other monotheistic religion (referring to Judaism and Christianity).

One of the major factors that need to be separated is the guidance of Islam as religion and the prevalence of traditional practices as well as perceptions rooted in different Muslim societies. It is of paramount importance to distinguish those factors to underline the dissemination of biased media reports that are not only selective in material but are also un-contextual as well as inaccurate. Islam as a religion gives an impressive array of claims to women. In addition to its spiritual side, Islam plays a regulating part in Muslim societies. The Islamic law, Sharia, tackles all matters relevant to society, from the smallest to the largest. Women's rights in all aspects of life have been addressed, as well as safeguarded and, if women were knowledgeable of their rights in Islam, they would be in a position of strength as well as enlightenment However, the important question that arises is whether Islamic law has been sufficiently exercised by the Muslim states, or for that matter, by some of the Muslim men. It is a fact that most Muslim states often engage a blend of traditional and Islamic, as well as some of the jurisprudence that has been inherited from the colonialists. In essence, there is great difference between Muslim states and Islamic states. Furthermore, it has been the case that some men continue to select verses in the Qur'ān whilst disengaging the sections that are not favourable to their argument in order to sway their propositions. For instance, it is also a Hadith that "To seek knowledge is duty for every Muslim (male) and every Muslim (female). Universal education both for men and women thus became the sacred law of Islam thirteen centuries before it was adopted by the civilisation of the west". [164] Yet there are Muslim and non-Muslim societies alike who prefer in times of scarce resources to send their sons to schools rather then daughters.

Contextually, therefore, many women activists in the west are very much concerned and angered that their achievements have not been recognised.

In Africa, once a continent of queens who ruled and influenced powers of the time, people are barely knowledgeable about that part of their history. Equally, in most parts of the Muslim and the Arab world, the historical perspectives of women leaders are not highlighted, but are neglected.

Therefore, without losing sight of the need to protect women's rights, locally regionally and globally and the cross-culture solidarity needed amongst women, one should be careful in separating politically motivated gestures from genuine concerns to extending helping hands. The major threat to women in the developing countries, Muslim and non-Muslims alike, does not originate from their male folks, but from bad policies that lead to conflicts, poverty, resultant problems, environmental and health hazard factors. As well as wars of conquest and conflicts, taking note that abusive husbands or partners are not faith-based but behaviour-deficient and universally oriented suggests that insight into specific cultures and religions out-weights the realities and is banyan pretence!

Conclusion

The Arab predicament is simply geographical. The UK and the US coalition forces are in Iraq, the Israelis in Palestine and both are occupying Arab lands. There may well be an Arab government that chooses to remain pragmatic towards the policies of the US and UK; but as far as the Arab public are concerned, if they leave and the occupation ends, then there will be peace. If the occupation continues, then it seems that some of the people would be compelled to continue to adopt desperate measures of supreme courage. With regard to Muslim countries and if they threaten western interests, in a stark contrast, there is ample evidence that suggests the opposite. For example, the British were, among other places, in Somalia, Palestine and Iraq, which are the hotbeds of the present-day Muslim World. In other words, it was Britain that ceded Somali territories to Kenya and Ethiopia, created the occupation of Palestine and did meddle with the Shia Sunni and Kurdish apparatus in Iraq and neighbouring regions. As early as 1956, the first peacekeeping operation was authorised by the Security Council under leadership of then Secretary-General Dag Hammarskjold that resulted in the attack of Egypt by France, the United Kingdom and Israel when Egypt tried to nationalise the Suez Canal. It was uniquely created for the Suez crisis and has no legal foundation in the United Nations Charter. In the Gulf region, the then Foreign Secretary Selwyn Lloyd stated that Britain must at all costs maintain control of that oil as a vital prize for any power interested in world influence or domination. So the British continued substantially to dominate the Gulf region's economy. The French were in Algeria. There were American air strikes against Iran, Sudan and Libya prior Bush's administration. The US was in Somalia in 1994 and after thirteen years returned to bombard southern Somalia. The US AC 130 gunship destroyed villages in an indiscriminate manner for several consecutive days. Even the Somali nomads, their livestock and grazing terrain, including forests, haven't been spared; the justification being that the US was after a so-called terrorist who allegedly bombed USA Embassies in Nairobi and Dar es-Salaam. Ironically, the American wanted men were not even Somalis, but the Somali country and Somali people had to pay the price. Moreover, the US was in Beirut in the 1980s so were the Israelis. Britain, the US and some of the NATO forces are in Afghanistan. Sanctions against Iran, the introduction of UN forces to the Sudan and Lebanon is yet another matter. Syria is periodically threatened. In terms of scholarships, the Muslims hardly engage strategic and political socio-economic studies to dismember the advancement of the "other". Just imagine if there were Muslim institutions funded and maintained by the state who were constantly to remind you how the USA is heterogeneous, how a Jewish president in the White House is not acceptable, how a Jew wasn't allowed membership to the tennis clubs in the US not long ago or the power struggle between those of Irish descent and the Americans from mainland Europe. What about the black Americans who remain at the periphery on the US economy, an economy that their ancestors worked so hard for? What about assisting the Irish when the English, used to hang the Irishman if he spoke his language, or how a Welsh candidate failed to occupy the position of the prime minister in Westminster or conspiracy against the union between the Scots and the English? Note that, after its 300th anniversary, who is disadvantaged in the union and how can divorce be sought? Imagine also if you were helped not to forget how Napoleon invaded England. If there is no love lost between the British and the French, what about the socio-economic barriers and disparities between classes and so on and so forth? That is usually the case in the "South" and it is mystifying when some of the western media engage in language like the animosity between the Shia and Sunni is centuries old, this community or that community is "complex" or "ambiguous" etc. Conversely, there is no country that does not acquire a history of clashes between and within communities. The differences are that there are no magnifying agencies from the developing world. In contrast, there are western institutions of diverse natures that habitually subscribe to fostering the tribal, religious, sectarian and border affiliations, such hair-splitting provisions that contribute to civil strife, undermine national cohesion and ultimately fence-in the virtues of human economic development. For example, a report prepared for the US State Department by the former US Ambassador to Ethiopia and Somalia, Professor David Shinn, entitled "Somalia: Regional involvement and implications for US policy", was commented upon by analysts as follows: "The Horn version of Great Game is much more serious than the cloak-and-dagger stuff of imperial espionage and diplomacy that pitted Czarist Russia against the British Empire in the period between 1813 and 1907 in central Asia. Rarely before in post-colonial Africa have we seen such an intense regional power struggle to shape the destiny of a country?" In simple language, there are those who prefer a united Somalia, return of the state and respect for Somali sovereignty and those who narrate a prelude that it is against their interest to see a strong Somalia once again, so they cultivate clan distinctions to hinder national consciousness. One UN employee in Kenya for Somali programmes commented, "The advantage with Somalia is, there is no government to restrict one's research".

In short, the position of the Muslims at this stage is defensive not offensive and historically it has been urban terrorism and guerrilla warfare that drove colonial powers out of the colonies, whether in Africa, Asia, Europe or beyond. The fate of neo-imperialism will not be any different. The US founding fathers, fleeing from religious persecutions in Europe and the Pilgrims were expected to have known better. Equally, the Jewish people, who have experienced aggression and genocide from the Romans, Christian Byzantium and Hitler's gas chambers, should bear in mind that no nation can be easily extinguished. Palestinians will not disappear just as the Jewish people didn't. The bottom line is that it is unwise to cultivate animosity. You may not know who will harvest it. All in all, it is recommendable to the west in general and the US, UK and Israel in particular to engage in a study that can enable them; a power not derived from the disempowerment and the destabilisation of the "other". Lessons are to be learnt from some of the European countries that advanced and developed in many areas without the peril of the gun. Some observers argue that the American empire building might have been more successful through Coca-Cola, MacDonald's, jeans and the film industry than the US gunship. Since the invasion of Iraq and Afghanistan, what the coalition of the willing introduced to the citizens of the globe, perhaps, is the normalisation of barbarity and piracy. The hanging of Sadam Hussein echoes when the crusades use to return with the heads of Turks, but, indeed, Bush told us, "this is a crusade war". In such a scenario, what one envisages is that civilisations are not clashing but enlightenment is evolving and the centre of intellectuality may return to the East sooner than anticipated. On the other side of the coin, one may argue that, as civilisation came from the East and it was the Arabs and Muslims who brought knowledge and so on to the West, is the West capable of passing it on or is it going to be the end of it all?

As for using cultural determinism to explain economic development, there have been earlier attempts. "A century ago Max Weber (1930) presented a major thesis on the decisive role of the Protestant ethic (in particular, Calvinism in the successful development of capitalist industrial economy). Weber's analysis of the role of culture in the emergence of capitalism drew on the world as he observed it in the late 19th century. His analysis is of particular interest in the contemporary world, especially in light of the recent success of market economies in non-Protestant societies. Theories of cultural determinism have often been one step behind the real world". These theories may provide some insight and lessons to be learnt.[165] the powers of today's world have to explore how to share the existing wealth and potential resources of the Muslim and non-Muslim worlds without presenting to them everlasting wars. It is indeed wisdom that brings modesty.

In terms of the US as a mono-power, anybody with a discerning eye could see that the Bush administration is not winning the Iraqi battle and will not prevail against the Somalis and the Afghanis. President Bush himself, when asked by the NBC US television whether America could win its "war on terror", replied "I don't think you can win it, but I think you can create conditions so that those who use terror as a tool are less acceptable in parts of the world". Indeed the US under the leadership of Bush is certainly less acceptable in many parts of the world. Therefore, the fiasco that follows the invasion of Iraq, both in the execution of the war and its legality, will have greater impact on future diplomacy and in many ways the respectability and the credibility of the US as defender of world peace, security and democracy may be contested. The destruction of Iraq may very much cement for the decline of the only super-power.

In the case of Islam and the argument that Muslim communities pose a threat to the West, so far has not been substantiated convincingly and not legally established. In many cases the reverse has been the case since 11/09/001. The challenge against that is growing and gaining momentum.

There is great difference between nationalistic endeavour that merits factual historical background, so closely linked with popular movements and players who engage national liberation movements and that sort of often propagated jihad, referred to as outright racism. Despite the vigorous attack on Islam in many ways, there has not been a success to identify any Islamist group whose argument wasn't based on the issues of injustice in the region and the problem of equity. In short, one must differentiate between the historically disadvantaged groups and "those that are motivated by ideology of cultural supremacy".

Islam is a fast-growing religion. On the whole, there are those who argue that there has not been aggressive Islamisation in concept and, indeed, in methodology as compared to different segments of the born-again Christians. It is worth noting that in India the Hindus and the Bahas are profoundly concerned about poverty-driven under-age Christianisation, to the extent that one Baha professor recommends that such actions of converting poor children from their born faiths should be regarded as human rights abuse.

When it comes to faith-swapping dynamism however, especially in the case of adults, and the traffic in self-search, soul-enhancement and cross-religious rhythm; these issues are beyond government prescriptions.

In the theme of the changing world, fears and concerns of power shifts, one does not need to be an enlightened philosopher to acknowledge that the world was never static. Throughout history powers were emerging while others weakened or faded.

It is of paramount importance, however, to drop what is largely regarded as self-inflected fear.

There are also the human connections, cross-faith and cultural relations that transcend political arrangements and geographical boundaries that contribute to peace building and these are not to be neglected. It is worth noting that, in 2003, London experienced the largest demonstration in its history against the Iraq war. One friend told me that if it had not been from the British public, Blair may have been even worse then he already exhibited.

Nonetheless, one could suggest that there is a need to explore bringing together experts of different faiths, scholars and intellectuals of positive minds, leaders of good intentions, opinion makers and human rights activists including the grass roots. Heads roll but come out with solutions that are diversity-based, humanly friendly and, to determine that globalisation should not equate to homogenisation, multiculturalism should prevail. They should promote world harmony and inclusiveness. In effect, universality should not mean the hidden agenda of neo-imperialism. There is difference between tolerance and respect, integration and assimilation and, perhaps, prejudice and racism.

Whilst the issues are not out of hand yet, there is a need to engage a body of independent international jurists and legal expert volunteers to adopt the case, to search the connections between Islam and terrorism and to safeguard and represent the interests of all at both international and national levels. Incitement to hatred may not only be selectively applicable to the less powerful. Normalisation of cruelty must be challenged across cultures, communities and faiths. Interdependence is a global factor for the world today and no one is immune to its drawbacks.

The Rewards of Success [1]

The Rewards of Success, from the classical Somali poetry, was composed by Ismail Mire, a Somali who was one of Sayyid Mohammad Abdullah Hassan's military commanders and the leader of the Dervish forces at the battle of Dulmadoba in the then British Somaliland, was composed shortly after the disappearances of Sayyid Mohammad in 1921. These verses were addressed, pointed in the final stanza, to the leader of a unit of Somali police engaged in restoring order amongst the Dhulbahante clan. The Somali policeman in question was, according to the poet, abusing his position to amass wealth at the expenses of the public. Such misuse of power leads to disaster as surely as pride always goes before a fall. This is the theme of the poem: it is illustrated by a series of cautionary examples, the characters in which are explained in the Notes. This poem is translated by late professor Andrewjewiski and Professor I.M. Lewis.

The word pride is described as dignity, honour, self-esteem, arrogance, bigheadedness but in this context the Somali word *kibir* could mean arrogance!

1 The Lord divides the bread amongst all his slaves
2 Taking care of the fishes in the sea and even of the contents of a cup.
3 Everyone will receive what has been prescribed for him;
4 Even though he runs fast or sets out early in the morning or climbs a high hill
5 No one will gain more than his allotted portion: let that be remembered!
6 It was to his overweening worldly pride that Corfield[2] owed his death; (I alone own the world)
7 It did not occur to him that young lads could kill with their rifles
8 Oh men, pride brings disaster: let that be remembered!

---

[1] This poem has been translated by Professor B.W. Andrzejewski and I M Lewis.
[2] Line 6&7 recall the death of Richard Corfield at the battle of Dul Madoba between the British and the Dervish forces in 1913.

9 He who drinks joyfully from the cup of prosperity and owns a
   herd of milk-camels

10 will surely lose his good fortune as it is written.

11 The whole Hagar[3] people were brought to ruin by the claim 'I
   am the king';

12 Oh men, pride brings disaster; let that be remembered!

13 Ina Galayd[4] repented of his words in the end;

14 There would have been no trouble had he brought the she
   camel,

15 He whom Ina Galayd despised would not then have pierced his
   kidneys with a spear.

16 Oh men, pride brings disaster; let that be remembered!

17 The six groups of Ali Geri[5] who almost destroyed each other

18 Failed to understand the words: 'This is watering trough and
   we can mend it ourselves.'

19 Oh men, pride brings disaster; let that be remembered!

20 In Amman's[6] worldly pride won him a whole land,

21 But he was without fear and did not expect to be killed by the
   man who assassinated him.

22 Oh men pride brings disaster; let that be remembered!

23 When 'Artan'[7] hung saddle on the tamarisk tree,

24 The Garaad Faarah lineage were as soft to him as a milk

---

[3] Line 9, 10&11, refers to a series of defeats by the Hagar lineage of the
Dhulbahante clan after a period of great prosperity which had led them to be
proud and boastful.

[4] Line 13,14 & 15, Galayd had twelve sons, one of his sons killed a man when
his lineage were collecting the hundred camels due in to compensation for the
death he refused to make any contribution and Ina Galayd's section was
defeated and he himself was executed.

[5] Here the reference is to fierce internecine strife which broke out among all
the six segments of the 'Ali Geri lineage of the Dulbahante clan following
trivial quarrel over precedence in a watering at a well. The quarrel started
when one man drove his spear through the watering trough of another as he
was waiting to water his stock.

[6] Lines 20&21 refer to a successful career of conquest, abruptly terminated
when the leader, Ina Ammaan of the 'Ainanshe lineage of the Habaryunis
clan, was murdered by someone against whom no precautions had been
taken and from whom aggression was not expected.

[7] Lines 23,24 &25 summarise the fortunes of 'Artan, agreat warrior. Such was
his reputation for bravery that mere sight of his saddle perched on the
branches of a tree was sufficient to keep the enemy at bay. Yet at last the
Garaad Faarah his enemies, plucked up courage and engaged 'Artan and his
kin in battle 'Artan lost his life.

sweat and sour,

25 But when battle was joined at last they became to him as bitter as poison.

26 Oh men pride brings disaster: let that be remembered!

27 Again and again the Sayyid[8] made war and people helped him;

28 Thousands upon thousands, all with white turbans, he brought to the battle of Beerdiga,

29 But what brought his downfall was the day when he destroyed the Khayr people.

30 Oh men, pride brings disaster: let that be remembered!

31 I saw a man such as those described who will not live long to enjoy his wealth,

32 He is full, satiated, and has grown fat buttocks like a big ram,

33 His bags are full of looted taken from men of honour and valour.

34 Watch silently, Muslims, and see how those who prosper lose their souls!

---

[8] In lines 27,28&29, The poet attributes the ultimate downfall of the Dervish movement to the Sayyid's wanton attack on the Khayr section of the Dulbahante clan. This lineage is composed largely of men of religion whom Somalis consider to be under Divine protection.

The Somali version of the Ismail Mire Cilmi's Poem.

Ismaaciil Mire Cilmi. Abwaanku wuxuu ka mid aha Abbaanduulayaashii Sayid Maxamed Cabdille Xasan. Wuxuu doorar lama illaawaan taariikhi ah ka soo qaatay dagaaladii Daraawiishtu kala horjeeday gumeysigii Ingiriska. Goobuhuu ugu waaweyna oo uu ku can baxay waxaa ka mid ahaa, dagaalkii Dulmadoobe. Halkaas, Ismaaciil Mire iyo ciidanku hoggaminayey waxay ku dileen taliyihii ciidankaa Ingiriska watay, Koofil(Richard Corfield), 1913. Gabaygani, wuxuu ka mid yahay maansooyinka sooyaalka Soomaaliyeed oo xigmadda ama fasafadda ku fadhiya kuwa ugu culus. Tixdu waxay xambaarsan tahay dhacdooyin iyo qisooyin ka dhacay abwaanku deegaankuu ku noolaa. Wuxuu gabaygan tiriyey burburkii Daraawiish ka dib, isagoo waayadaa magaalo ku soo laabtay oo hoos yimid maamulkii iyo taliskii Ingiriska.

Carab Cawaale Jaamac (Carab Dheere) oo ceelka Laascanood Ingiriisku maamule uga dhigay, aya u sabab ahaa in Ismaaciil Mire tixdan curiyo, Gabyaagu wuxuu arkay Saajin Carab Dheere oo awoodiisii si aad u foolxun oo xad dhaaf ah ugu tagrifalay. Waxanu yidhi:

Inkastuu kallaho ama kabtiyo, ama kur dheer fuulo
Bad kalluun ku jira kay ku tahay, amase koob shaaha
Kulligood addoomaha Rabbow, qaybshay kimistiiye
Nin waliba wixii loo katibay, waa la kulansiine
Ninna inaanu soo korodhsanayan, kaa ha la ogaado!
Anaa dunida keligey leh buu, koofil eersadaye
Kashiisaba ma gelin wiilal baa, keebka kuu qabane
Ragow kibirka waa lagu kufaa kaa ha la ogaado!

Ninkii koob nimco ah fuuqsada, kadin irmaan maala
In karuurka uu qubo horey, kaafka ugu tiile
Kulligoodba Reer Hagar anaa kiin ahaa dilaye
Ragow, kibirka waa lagu kufaa kaa ha la ogado!

Ammuurah ma kaadsado ninkay, kado shidaysaaye
Kalaamkuu lahaa Ina Gallaydh, kahay gadaalkiiye

Kaarkuba ma joogeen hadduu, keeno tuluddiiye
Baallacad kelyaha kuma jareen, kii uu quudhsadaye
Ragoo kibirka waa lagu kufaa, kaa ha la ogaado!

Lixda koose Reer Cali Gariye, kaw isga siiyey
Kasi waaye wuxu waa qabaal, waana kabannaaye
Ragow kibirka waa lagu kufaa, ka ha la ogaado!

Kaysaha adduun Ina Ammaan, kama qarraacnayne
Ragba keeno geli buu is yidhi, waad u korraysaaye
Isba kii arsaa'ilay ma hadin, kamana yaabayne
Rago kibir ka waa lagu kufaa, kaa ha la ogaado

Kelyo caano galeen baa ninkii, kiciye dheereeye
Cartan dhuurta kooraha markuu, kor ugu laalaayay
Garaad Faarax dhay iyo karuur, kal macaanaye
Misna kala qadhaadha dhunkaal, kulanki goobeede
Ragow kibirka waa lagu kufaa, kaa ha la ogaado!

Kufri iyo Islaam loo collow, kaysihii hora'e
Kaakici wadaadkii jahaad, laguna kaalmeeye
Kumanyaal lag wada duubcad buu, keenay Beerdhiga'e
Waxse kadabkii go'ay markii uu, kaday raggiisiiye
Kabaalkina wuxuu jaby kolkuu,kariyey Reer Khayre
Rago kibirka waa lagu kuaa. Kaa ha la ogaado!

Nin kuwaa ka dhigan baan arkaa, kadab u laabnayne
Karraysaha intu buuxsaday oo, Kaman wan weyn yeeshay
Yuu niman karaamiyo colba leh, kiish ka buuxsadaye
Ka shib dhaha Islaamow naftii, kii ladnaa gadaye!

141

Endnotes

1. Wallerstein Immanuel: Africa and the Modern World. Africa World Press Inc. Trenton: new Jersey, US 1986 p17

2. Human Development Report: Cultural Liberty in Today's Diverse World: by United Nation Development Programme. New York, 10017 USA. 2004 P27

3. Ibid. p.27

4. Kishore Saint: Conflict Resolution in the Context of Development Induced Ecological and Livelihoods Degradation. Unpublished paper for the conference towards harmony: Conflict Resolution and Reconciliation. Indira Gandhi National Centre for Arts Dec 17 to 20 2004 New Delhi P1

5. Ibid. p.1

6. Ibid Gandian Frame of Action P2

7. Stiglitz Joseph. Former Chief Economist of the World Bank. Essay Titled "The Hospital that makes you sicker". New internationalist P14

8. Op.cit. Waller Immanuel P183

9. Richard Burton: First Footsteps in Africa, An Exploration of Harrar Volume 1, published by Darf publishers 1894, 1986,   P82

10. A.M Brocket. The British Somaliland to 1905: Thesis Lincoln College, Oxford, 1965.p14

11. Somaliland Foreign Affairs Dispatches. No.6 Mr. Rodd to Marques of Salisbury, received May 1897

12. See Harrar Conference, Confidential Report on the Somaliland, Ethiopia Harar Dec.1955-January, 1956

13. Anatomy of Third World Cold War Crisis: Horn of Africa, 1977-78: Cold War International History Project Bulletin Issue 8-9, p35

14. Ibid p38

15. Jeffery A. Lefebure: Arms for the Horn, U.S –Security Policy in Ethiopia and Somalia 1953 –1991.Published in University of Pittsburgh Press 1991 p242

16. Deborah L. West: Combating Terrorism in the Horn of Africa and Yemen .World Peace Foundation Report. Conference held on November 4-6, 2004. p1

17. Ibid p6

18 Ibid p16
19. Ibid p17
20. Ibid p20
21. Ibid p20
22. Ibid p 18
23. Ibid p 14
24. Ibid p14
25. Ibid p19
26. See the Observer, London, 11, April, 2004, p 29
27. See, the Asian Security Summit in Singapore June 2003
28 See, the Guardian, London, 9 April, 2004, p24
29 The Guardian, London, 9 December 2004, p17
30. George A. Lopez & David Cortright: Trouble in the Gulf, Pain and Promise. May/June 1998 PP 40, 41, 42
31 Plant People the Ecologist. May 2004 p40
32 See, the Third World Resurgence issues No 151, 152 Jan 2004, p50
33 Ibid p50
34. Ibid p51
35. See the Financial Times. London, June 26/27, 2004, p7
36. See, the Times London 15 May 2004 pp27
37. Ibid pp22
38. Opcit, Third World Resurgence Magazine, Issue No 151-152, 1/o4 p55.
39. Opcit, the Guardian. London. 9 April 2004, p24
40. Munoz Heralad, Ambassador of Chile: The Rising Right to Democracy in America, Unpublished Paper
41. See, the Independent London 11 April 2005 pp25
42. Mernissi Fatima: the Forgotten Queens of Islam. Policy Press 1993. First published in France pp185
43. See Newsweek April 19/26 2004 pp34
44. See the Plant and People the Ecologist May 2004 pp4
45. See Human Right Watch Report on Iraq Dec 203
46. See Respect News Pullet March 2005
47. See Observer London. 11 July 2004, p27
48. RI-Hon Michael Portillo, Democratic value and the single currency. Lecture given to the Institute of Economic Affairs. Church house, Westminster.19 Jan 1998 pp28
49. Opcit. Third World Resurgence issue no 151-152 1, Jan 20o4, p 21

50. Ibid p 22
51. Ibid p 69
52. Opcit Human Right Watch report on Iraq
53. Opcit Third world Resurgence issue no 151-152. 1 –Jan
    2004 pp 22
54. Ibid pp22
55. Ibid pp23
56. Ismail Raji al- Faruqi: Islam and the other Faiths, Published
    by the Islamic Foundation UK 1998, p87
57. See Guardian London, 10 Dec, 2004, p28
58. See Guardian London, 21, Sept, 2004, p25
69. See Guardian London 9 Dec, 2003, p1
60. Opcit Ismail Raji al-Farugi pps, 34, 35
61. The Last Two Million Years: Published by the Reader's
    Digest Association, printed in Britain 1973, p 406
62. Ibid pps 405, 46
63. Ncomparisonew radio
64. Opcit The Last Two Million Years, p406
65. Al-Ahram weekly web@ahram.org.eg, See Workers News
    Service April 19, 2001: Dr. George Habash Statement.
66. Middle East Stage Dr. Hanan Ashrawi http:
    www.worldtrek.orgodysseymideast / ashrawibio
67. See, the Independent London, 27, Sept, 2003, p17
68. See, the Guardian, 7, Sept, 2004, p16
69. Ibid p 16
70. See, The Guardian. London/Manchester 28 August 2004
    pp22
71. See, the Guardian 7 Oct 2004 pp18
72. See, the Observer 18 July 2004 pp18
73. See, the Guardian 3, Sept 2004, p8
74. See, the Metro London, 14March, 2005, p5
75. See, the Independent, 11, April, 2005, p13
76. See, the Guardian, July 16, 2004, P4
77. See, the Guardian, July 16, 2004, p4
78. See, the Guardian, London, July, 10, 2004, P1
79. See, the Observer, London, 18, July, 2004, P4
80. See, the Guardian, London, 2, August, 2004, P2
81. See, the Guardian, London, 24, April, 2004, P22
82. See, the Guardian, London, August, 9, 2004, P9
83. See, the Guardian, 7, September, 2004, P 27

84. Norwich Julus John: Byzantium, The Early Centuries published by Guild Publishing, London 1998, pps127,135,136.

85. Gibbon Edward: The Decline and Fall of the Roman Empire, 1993,Afred Knoff, Volume 1,2,3,p31

86. See, the New Internationalist, 356, May, 2003, P34

87. The last Two Million Years, Readers Digest: Published by Readers Digest Association, London, New York, Sydney, Cape Town, P 126.

88. Opcit: New Internationalist, 356, May, 2006, P6

99. Ibid: P6

90. Ibid: P6

91. Opcit: The Third World, Resurgence Issue, No, 151-152, January, 2004, P 30

92. (See more on unclassified documents JCS /1969? 321, 12 march 1962 page2165 Cuba project)

93. Opcit: Third World Resurgence, Jan, 2004, P22

94. See, the New York Times, 7, December 2004

95. Anthony Nutting: No End of a Lesson, The inside Story of the Suez Crisis, 1967, published by Clarkson, Potter, inc, New York, USA, P118

96. Ibid 126-127

97. See the Guardian, London, July, 16, 2004, P18

98. Opcit: New Internationalist 356 May, 2003, P33

99. See, the Mail, London, 9, May 2004

100. See, the Guardian, London, August, 12, 2005, P22

101. See, the Financial Times, May, 22/23/ 2004, P18

102. Opcit: Kishore Saint, unpublished paper

103. Opcit: The Last Two million Years, P50

104. Ibid: P54

105. Ibid: P54

106: Ibid: PPs 54, 55

107: Ibid: PPs, 151, 152

108. Ibid: PPs, 48, 50

109. Muhammad Marmaduke. Pickthall: Cultural Side of Islam, First Published in 1927 New Delhi, P21

110. Ibid PPs 68, 69

111: Opcit, the Last two Million Years, P 157

112: Ibid: P157

113: Ibid: P54

114: Ibid P 152

115: Ibid P151

116: Opcit Cultural Side of Islam, P 32

117: Opcit: The Last Two Million Years, P 157

118: R.A.Jairasbhoy: Influence of Islamic Architecture in Western Europe. Arts &the Islamic world volume 1 no 1, Dar Ala Islam Geneva 1983 Switzerland P25

119: Mernissi Fatima: The Forgotten Queens of Islam, Polity Press 1993, p23

120: Opcit: The last Two Million Years, P 154.

121: See the Observer, London, June, 6, 2004, P14

122: Opcit, the Last Two Million Years, P70

123: Ibid: P65

124: Ibid P82

125: I. A. Ibrahim: A Brief Illustrated Guide to Understand Islam, Second Edition, Published by Darussalam Houstan, 1997, 1996, PPs 10, 11

126: Ibid, P11

127: Ibid P14

128: Opcit, Cultural Side of Islam, Ps 21, 22

129: Ahmed Deedat: Islam and Christianity, Volume One, South Africa, 1993, pps 9, 10

130: Opcit: The Last Two Million Years, P87

131: Ibid: P405

132: Opcit; Ahamed Deedat, PPs 10, 11

133: Ibid: P117

134: Ibid: P116

135: Franklin H, littell: Historical Atlas of Christianity, 1997, 2001, P84

136: Ibid: P83

137: Ibid: 83

138: Ibid: 83

139: Abdulrahman A. Sheeha: Women In the Shadow of Islam, Riyadh, Saudi Arabia, 1997, P10

140: Ibid P11

141: Ibid, P20

142: ibid: PPs 19, 20

143: Ibid: P18

144: Ibid: P15

145. Ibid: P54

146. Ibid: P2
147. Ibid P2
148. Ibid, P35
149. Ibid P1
150. Ibid P6
151. Ibid P4
152. Ibid P9
153. Opcit, Mernissi Fatima, P14
154. Ibid, P14
155. Ibid, P16
156. Ibid, P19
157, Trimingham J. Spencer: Islam in Ethiopia, Frankcass, London, 1952, P115
158. See Metro. London, May 1, 2003, p7
159. Violence against Women in the United States .Source A National crime victimization Survey Report US Department of Justice Washington, D.C January 1994 http/www.Now.Org
160. See the Observer London, March, 6, 2004, P18
161. Ibid: P18
162. See the Guardian, London, December, 7, 2004, P3
163. See the Guardian London, July, 31, 2004, P1
164 Opcit: Cultural Side of Islam P11
165. Op. cit: Human Development Report, (UNDP) USA, 2004

Bibliography

Books. Papers and unpublished Material

A.K Merchant: A statement by the National Spiritual Assembly of
    Bahais of India Communal Harmony India's greats
    Challenge 1991 Bahai Publishing Trust New Delhi India

B.W. Andrzejewski and I M Lewis, *Somali Poetry: An*
    Introduction, Oxford Clarendon Press, 1964

Bahn Paul G. The Story of Archaeology, 1996, George
    Weidenfeld & Nicolson Ltd. London.

Bray, Clarke & Stephens, Education and Society in Africa, 1986,
    Edward Arnold ltd, London.

Cotterell A, the Minoan World, 1979; Michael Joseph Ltd,
    London.

Deacon Richard, Escape, the Mogadishu Hijack, 1980, British
    Broadcasting Corporation, London.

Deedat Ahmed, The Choice, Islam and Christianity volume one,
    1993, Ebi Lockhat, South Africa.

Farsy Fouad Al, Saudi Arabia A Case Study in Development,
    1986, Kegan Paul International Limited, London.

George A. Lopez and David Cortright: The Trouble in the Gulf
    Pain and Promises. May/June 1998 pps41 42

Gibbon Edward, the Decline and fall of the Roman Empire
    (volume 1, 2 and 3); 1993; Alfred A.Knopf, Inc.

Grant M, the Rise of the Greeks, 1987; Guild Publishing London

Heraldo Munoz, Ambassador of Chile, the Rising Right to
    Democracy in the Americas. Organization of American States
    Washington D.C The Views presented the idea of
    Sovereignty

Hildegarde Kiwasila: Institute of Resource Assessment,
    University of Dar-es-salm.

Hourani Albert, a History of the Arab Peoples, 1992, Harvard
    University Press, New York.

Huntington S, The Clash of Civilisations and the Remaking of
    World Order, 2002; Free Press UK Ltd.

Ibrahim Al-Aqidi: PhD Thesis, The Iraqi Army and politics 1941-
    1953, University of Exeter 1989.

Ismail Raji al-Faruqi, Islam and the other faiths published by the Islamic foundation 1998 United Kingdom

Kapchits Georgi, the Dictionary of Somali Proverbs, 1998, Vostochnaya Literatura Publishers, Moscow.

Kondepudi Lavanya, a Gifted Life, 2003, Sona Printing Press, Munirka.

Lawrence T.E, Seven Pillars of Wisdom, 1962, Penguin Group, London.

M. M. Picthal: Cultural Side of Islam, Published First in India 1927

Mernissi Fatima, the Forgotten Queens of Islam, Polity press 1993

R.A. Jairasbhoy: Oriental influence in the western Art, Asia publishers House 1965

Rice M, Egypt's Making-The Origins of Ancient Egypt 5000-2000BC, 1990; Guild Publishing London

Sadat Jehan, a Woman of Egypt, 1987, Bloomsbury Publishing ltd, London.

Said Edward W, Orientalism, 2003; Penguin Group London.

Said, Edward W; Power, Politics and Culture, 2004, Bloomsbury Publishing Plc. London

Shorouk Darl El, Forth Hadith Qudsi, H.H Sheikh Zayed bin Sultan Al Nahayan, 2nd Edition.

The Last Two Million Years, 1973; the Readers Digest Association, London.

Trimingham J.Spencer: Islam in Ethiopia, Published by Francass, London 1952.

Wallerstein Immanuel, Africa and the Modern World, Africa World Press, 1996, New Jersey

Wilson Hilary, People of the Pharaohs, 1999, Brockhampton Press.

RT Hon Michael Portillo: Lecture given to the institute of Economic Affairs, Church House Westminster London, P 4

Papers presented by Dr. A.K Merchant, Dr. S.K.Pachaure, Dr. Rudolf C. Heredia and Professor Modjtaba Sadria: Papers presented at the International Conference towards Harmony Conflict Resolution and Reconciliation. December 2004, New Delhi, India.

Kishore Saint: Gandhian Frame of Action. Unpublished paper presented at the "International conference Towards Harmony conflict Resolution and Reconciliation New Delhi India. December 2004.

Violence against Women in the United States: Source: A National Crime Victimization Survey Report US Department of Justice, Washington, D.C. January 1994, http:/www.now.org

The Guardian, London, August 13th, 2004
The Times, London, May 15 2004,
The Guardian, London, July 17 2004.
The Guardian, London, March 5 2005
The Guardian , London, September13th, 2004
The Guardian, London, July 1st, 2004
The Guardian, London, July 10, 2004
The Guardian, London, July 16th, 2005
The Guardian, London, September 21st, 2004
The Observer, London, August 1st, 2004
The Guardian, London, August 13th, 2004
The Guardian, London, April 16th, 2005
The Times, London, May 15th, 2004
The Guardian, London, December 9
The Guardian, London, Friday 16th, 2004
The Observer, London, May 30th
The Observer, London, August 15th, 2004
The Guardian, London, July 9th, 2004
The Observer, August 9th, 2005
The Guardian , December 7th, 2004
The Guardian, September 6th, 2004
The Guardian, August 28th, 2004
The Independent, September 27th, 2003
The Guardian, July 1st, 2004
The Guardian, August 31st, 2004
The Guardian, July 16th, 2004
The Guardian, September 7th, 2004
The New York Times, November 16th, 2004
The Independent, April 11th, 2005
The Guardian, April 14th, 2004

The Observer, July 18th, 2004
The Observer, April 11th, 2004.
The Times London July 1,200

Index